EMBRACING THE WILD
IN YOUR DOG

An understanding of the authors of our dog's behavior-nature
and the wolf

Bryan Bailey

Published by FastPencil

I dedicate this book to God, the author of nature, wolves, dogs and man.

~

I dedicate this book to my mentor.
When I walk my final path into the wild and meet him there, I pray this book and the way I have lived my life, will earn his approval.

~

I dedicate this book to my beautiful wife, Kira.
She is my student, my hiking partner in the wild, and my best friend.
Without her, this book would never have been written, for while I was writing, she was taking care of life.

۶ی

Acknowledgments

I am well versed in the rules of nature and how they apply to social predators, but I obviously don't know the rules of grammar and how they apply to the written word! Many thanks to Lauren Riley for her contributions in editing and commenting on this book.

I would like to thank Dr. Thomas Slattery for his insight and willingness to partner with me in the ongoing use of pharmacotherapy to give maladaptive dogs a chance at a better quality of life.

Much appreciation to Dr. Joanna Jones. Standing on the opposite side of a surgery table for 10 years allowed me to cleave her vast knowledge of veterinary medicine. What I learned, I use every day.

Contents

Introduction

To look into the eyes of a wolf is to see your soul.
Just be sure something you want to view is there.
~ Iroquois saying

Ranger, my seven-year-old, male, Alaskan sled dog, is lying on the frozen ground chewing a stick when Scarlett, a new twelve-week-old female pup, cautiously noses up to him to investigate what he is chewing. Her inquiry is met immediately with a hard, deliberate stare that is accompanied by a low, menacing growl. Like an echo from a distant time when all aggression was sparked by competition for survival, Ranger's growl leaves no doubt as to the outcome if Scarlett fails to heed his warning.

Perhaps Scarlett has been deficiently socialized to powerful, dominant males such as Ranger, or perhaps up until this moment in life, she has always taken what she has wanted, but whatever the reason, she fails to retreat in the speed and manner required to avoid an attack. With an imperceptible speed, Ranger springs up, snatches Scarlett by the throat, and pins her to the ground. Suddenly, finding herself the replacement for the stick in Ranger's mouth, Scarlett flails and howls with every ounce of strength that her twelve weeks of life can bring to bear. Escape is not possible.

"If I do not wish to share, I won't!" is the lesson, and the teacher is a domestic wolf named Ranger. Drawing from a lesson plan created thousands of years ago by nature for the use of social predators, Ranger indoctrinates Scarlett on the way of the wolf where dominance prevails and submission yields. The force of his teeth on her neck does not crush her. His formidable muzzle chokes off her air, but he does not suffocate her. Ranger holds Scarlett firmly, pinned on her back, until she relinquishes her fight and becomes still. "I am Ranger, and to you, young one, my will is law. Yield to me," is said through the eyes of the unconquerable wolf that reigns in the heart of Ranger and in all domestic dogs. Then, he releases her.

The use of aggression to assert his will and to teach a valuable lesson to Scarlett would have horrified most pet owners, and Ranger would have most likely been punished for his unacceptable behavior while Scarlett would have been doted on for her near death experience. Worse yet, Scarlett may not have been allowed to be in the company of Ranger again for fear of her safety, and this action would have denied her access to the many important lessons that Ranger would have provided her in the future.

We humans would have intervened when nature would have acknowledged. We would have suppressed what nature would have blossomed. Like so many other things we do, we would have tried to change the unchangeable because we are human, and we are all powerful, and, unfortunately, we are all ignorant. Ranger's employment of an aggressive mechanism while maintaining control of his stick was as natural to him as your brushing your teeth. In his world, the world of wolves, his aggression was not only justifiable but also necessary to accomplish his inherited duty of educating and protecting the offspring of his species. Because we do not know or because we simply refuse to acknowledge that dogs' behaviors are more wolf-like than we wish them to be, we have endowed dogs with the same moral consciousness and rules of conduct that we would expect of ourselves and other decent humans. We would have shared our stick with Scarlett and would have expected her to share hers with us if she had one. We would not have kept our stick to ourselves like Ranger. We would have treated her like any other member of our family and would not have discriminated against her desire to achieve an equal status with us. We would not have pinned her to the ground like Ranger to emphasize our power and our authority over her. We would have taught her to ask, not take; too question, not yield; to assert, not submit. And sadly, there tips the first domino that leads to a relational discord with our dogs.

They're not humans, and they should not be treated like humans.

This is not a training book. However, I can't imagine attempting to properly train a dog without knowing the information presented in this book. It does not cover obedience topics such as heel, sit, down, stay, and come. Instead, it is about my growing up in the Alaskan wild under the tutelage and guardianship of a Special Forces survival instructor who introduced me to the ways of wolves and the similarities they share with dogs. It is about the wisdom and splendor of nature and the many life lessons she provides. Mostly, it is about developing a deep understanding of the authors of your dog's behavior—nature and the wolf. In doing so, you will truly learn who and what your dog really is and the whys and hows of its behavior. You will learn the tools that nature gave your dog to survive and coexist in both the wild and in your home. You will learn how activating and deactivating natural impulses and mechanisms in your dog will lead to the harmonious existence and the control you always dreamed of. Lastly, you will come to know the wolf in your dog and accept it for the wonderful gift that it is.

Lessons from the Wild

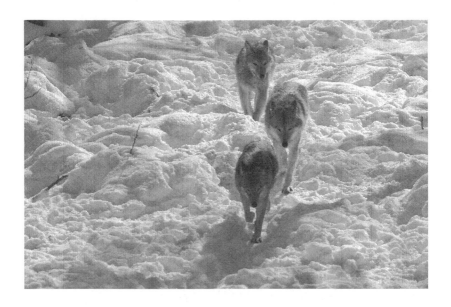

If a man is as wise as a serpent,
he can afford to be as harmless as a dove.
~ Cheyenne Proverb

"Do you know what you're looking at?" my mentor asks as he stands looking over my shoulder. "Wolf prints?" I answer timidly because I still had trouble differentiating between wolf and wolverine tracks.

"Yep. How many wolves left these prints?" he questions. Now he is squatting next to me, perfectly balanced on his snowshoes even though he is supporting a fifty-pound pack on his back. "I'm not sure," I reply, knowing that's not the answer my

mentor is looking for, but it's the truth. Telling the truth will earn me a lesser penalty than if I just make up a number.

"Not sure? Not sure doesn't work out here in the wild. Not sure gets you killed. Only being sure works, and being sure about how many wolves are near us is important.I'm going to go back over our trail a bit while you figure out how many wolves left these tracks. When you ARE SURE, let me know," he commands. With that, he taps me on my shoulder and heads back down the trail from which we had come.

As a young lad in Alaska, my introduction to wilderness survival and navigating the wild was not with the Boy Scouts but with my mentor, a U.S. Army Green Beret. Having been blessed with only two daughters, he took me under his wing, and I became the son he always wanted. Under his tutelage, weather patterns, terrain, foliage, animal behavior, and survival equipment were all broken down to their most basic forms and taught to me. He was a lean, muscular man with a square jaw and steel, gray eyes that never missed any mistake I made. The wild was his home, and he fit so perfectly in it that if I didn't know any better, I would have thought he had been born from mountain rock and suckled by a wolf. He was as mean as a wounded moose when he needed to be but as loving and protecting as a she-bear to her cubs at other times. He was Steve McQueen, Paul Newman, and Charles Bronson all wrapped up in one man. He was my hero, and I wanted nothing more than to be just like him.

Alaska is well known for her cold winters, and today is no exception. The bitter cold is playing havoc with my ability to concentrate. I keep catching myself trying to figure out how many usable toes and fingers I still have instead of how many wolves have traveled through the area. The days are also very short in the winter, and a quick glance at the horizon tells me I don't have much longer to solve my mentor's question.

I know the first part of the equation is to determine the speed of the wolves. Not only is my mentor sure to ask me this question, but the faster the wolves ran, the easier it was to count them.

Because nature at her most basic form is an exchange of energy for more energy, wolves usually travel at an energy-conserving trot, not at a gallop. While trotting, wolves leave an alternating track pattern where the hind leg's paw print often lands on top of the opposite front leg's paw print. This makes discerning the tracks of three or four wolves traveling together a cinch, but with wolves usually traveling in a single file while trotting, any number greater than this can almost be impossible to tell. However, in a gallop, such as what wolves use while chasing prey, the number of wolves is easier to tell because the wolves usually break off the disciplined single file trot line and fan out. This strategic move creates individual tracks that make it easy for a tracker to not only know how many wolves are involved in the hunt but also to know their approximate size and hierarchal status among the group. Even if the wolves do not fan out, the speed of some of the wolves will be greater than the others, and centrifugal force will push them off the established single file line to create individual tracks. I know this for a fact because this had to be compensated for when my dogs pulled my sled; otherwise, a crash was almost certain.

It doesn't take me long to figure out that lady luck isn't going to bless me with a group of galloping wolves today. These wolves are traveling single file, and there are layers and layers of tracks on top of tracks, meaning my most accurate hypothesis is not going to be a specific number but a bunch of wolves instead. I know I am going to receive a butt-chewing from my mentor, but trying to look on the bright side, I figure if he makes me do a hundred push-ups with my pack on for not getting the answer right, it will at least warm me up. Rationalizing that there is no need to prolong the inevitable, I set off down the trail to report the bad news to my mentor.

I had traveled far enough without finding my mentor to start wondering if he had decided to leave me out here on my own. It wouldn't have been much of a surprise if he had because he'd chosen to do so a few times before as a way of testing my ability to remain calm and get myself out of a precarious situation. On one particular occasion, we had driven over thirty kilometers from the base where we both lived and then had trekked another ten more into the wild when my mentor told me he needed to relieve himself. With that, he left me where I was and disappeared behind a stand of trees. Everything my mentor did was fast, including what he was doing then, so after about fifteen minutes when he hadn't reappeared, I became a little concerned and went looking for him. Behind the stand of trees, I did not find my mentor, but I did find a note tacked to one of the low hanging branches. It said, *"See you back home."* At least he thought enough to pull that one on me during the summer!

"What did you find out?" I hear as I about jump out of my skin. The man has an uncanny way of materializing out of nowhere, and I had still not gotten used to it. Watching him step out from behind a spruce tree, I answer, "I tried my best, sir, but I can't tell you exactly how many. They were trotting in a single file line, and there were tracks covering up tracks everywhere! But, I do know because of that, it has to be more

than you can shake a stick at." I give it to him straight. Heck, I'm so cold I figure, what is a little more misery going to do to me?

"So, approximately how many wolves do you figure you would be shaking that stick at?" he asks as he snaps a small branch off the tree he's standing next to. Pruning the branch until it's bare, he hands it to me and asks, *"What'syour best guess?"* This doesn't help me a bit. History has proven to me that when my mentor gives me permission to guess at something, it's like navigating through a minefield. Some answers provide clear passage while others blow up in my face. Geez, how can someone be so good at torture? "My best guess would be six to eight wolves, sir." Now it's time to find out if I live or die.

"Good guess. There are actually eight of them, and they're headed northwest of our location on a hunt," he replies, grinning. Well, at least I'm not going to die from something other than the cold, but, before I can celebrate, I surprise myself and ask him, "How in the world did you figure that out?" I'm amazed at both my brazenness for asking a master of the wild how he knows what he knows and the fact that he did know what he knew! I can definitely chalk this one up to a self-inflicted wound.

"Follow me, and I'll show you," he chuckles as he turns and leads me to where the wolves' tracks slow to a stop at the edge of a frozen pond. There he shows me where the wolves have split up in their attempt to find a crossing that will not require them to walk across the treacherous ice. Four of the wolves went north while four of them went south. The tracks laid by each individual wolf were spread apart just enough to count them accurately. I shake my head. Doubting the capabilities of

my mentor was as foolish as trying to stop a charging moose with a snowball. He was never in the wild—he was the wild.

"Don't look so amazed, kid. Nature will always provide you with what you seek. If you ever want to master the wild, you will have to accept this and trust in her ways. When you do learn to trust her, you won't need to guess anymore because she will reveal the answers to all the questions you ask." He pauses for a few moments while I think about what he has said. Then he goes on, *"Like you, the tracks told me there was a bunch of wolves headed somewhere. When I realized that, I remembered nature's lessons about wolf behavior. At this time of year, when a bunch of wolves travel together, they are looking for something to kill and eat. What are they looking to kill and eat? The large animals that hang out in the lower valleys during winter. Where is such a valley? Nature made one approximately six klicks northwest from here. Knowing this landscape, I knew the wolves would have to slow down for one reason or another, so I headed northwest and that's when I discovered this beaver pond and the split tracks."* It doesn't matter that he told me not to be amazed because I can't help but feel I am in the presence of one of the most incredible humans on earth. His ability to retain nature's lessons and then use them to problem-solve any situation still baffles me even though I have witnessed it a hundred times over.

"Why is it important that we know how many wolves there are and what they're up to?" he continues. I know this answer. I had observed wolves many times in the past, and I knew that a large kill would not be totally consumed by these eight wolves. I respond with, "In a survival situation in the wild, it is crucial to know where any source of water or food may be obtained. If this were a large group of wolves, we would know

they were hunting large game and if we were to follow this group, we may come across the remains of any successful kill they make. Because the animal they may kill will most likely be very large, the wolves will not consume everything and anything leftover could possibly feed us for days if needed." I feel good about my answer, and I wait for the praise that always came sparingly but was wanted as much as a man dying of thirst wants water. My mentor shifts his pack and stamps his snowshoes while he stares at me. He lets what is probably only a few minutes pass, but it is long enough for me to start doubting my answer. I nervously start stamping my own snowshoes and shifting my pack as well.

"So, kid. What if it had turned out those were wild dog tracks we were following and not wolves? Would your answer be any different?" he probes, stopping to stamp his snowshoes and shift his pack. He stands there with his hands on his hips waiting for my answer. The sun has dropped over the horizon, and the last orange rays backlight the man who has been and would be the biggest influence in my life. Making him proud of me will last more than this moment. It will last and sustain me for a lifetime. Picturing in my mind the time my lead sled dog Ranger gave chase to a large elk that had wandered into our backyard, I answer, "No sir. Dogs are wolves at heart, and they behave like wolves. I would have let their tracks lead me to food."

My mentor playfully cuffs me on the side of my head, and smiling, he says, *"Well, lucky for us, we won't have to follow those dogs tonight. Let's build a fire and heat up the food we brought."*

My answer was correct that day and is still correct now. Dogs are wolves at heart, and they behave like wolves. There's no need to guess anymore.

I learned many lessons during the years I spent with my mentor in the Alaskan wild. In all of them, I learned to trust nature and her ways and like my mentor said, she has always provided the answers to the many complex questions I have asked her. In the process, she has exposed my human frailty in contrast to her sovereign presence, my obvious naivety when compared to her all-knowing percipience and my demanding arrogance in opposition to her humble servility. She has been the master teacher, and she has made her presence known all throughout my life.

In writing this book, I relied upon the lessons my mentor and nature both taught me so that I may attempt to mentor you. I did not rely upon the teaching of others as they were not needed. Nature gave rise to wolves and dogs and bound them together with the everlasting thread of instinct; nature has passed this knowledge on to me. In the following chapters, I have done my best to share this knowledge in hopes that, like me, you will come to embrace the *wild* in your dog and the grace and the peace that is breathed into its acceptance.

The Path of Three Prints

And while I stood there, I saw more than I can tell,
and I understood more than I saw;
for I was seeing in a sacred manner
the shapes of things in the spirit,
and the shape of all shapes as they must
live together like one being.
~ Black Elk

She sat across from me twisting a tissue with hands that revealed a woman who had cared for her late husband and her many children. Embarrassed, she looked away as she occasionally dabbed at tears that wandered down her cheeks. I had seen this before, not with this woman, but with many others; yet, it still seemed like the first time, and it still hurt. After several minutes, she gathered herself and turned towards me, crumbled the tissue in her fist, and locked her gaze on me. At that moment, I knew she had changed. Tears and slumped shoulders were now replaced by hard, amber eyes and a rigid jaw, an obvious reflex of having survived many personal trials in her life. Pulling back her shoulders, she leaned forward, and without hesitation, she stated, "The right thing to do by my family is to put my dog to sleep, and that's what I'm going to do." Sighing, I settled back in my chair and wondered where this woman's generation had gone—a generation where the blue collar man was the backbone of an unheralded nation, where a handshake still meant something, and where suffering was accomplished with dignity and silence.

Just thirty minutes earlier, this woman had painfully explained why she had come to visit me. She told me about the recent passing of her beloved husband of fifty seven years. She told me that her husband adopted a shepherd-chow mix named Rex and how much the dog's playful nature had helped him cope with the illness that eventually claimed his life. She talked about how this dog was a living reminder of her husband and how much she cherished it, and about how this dog, the salvation of her loneliness, had inexplicably bitten her four-year-old grandson just two days earlier. Finally, she explained how the grandson's parents, fearing for their child's safety, threatened to never bring their son back to visit her again as long as Rex was alive.

"But why would Rex bite a harmless child and put me through the pain of having to do this? After all, he's known my grandson since he was a baby," she asked. Before I was able to answer, she pressed on, "This is my fault. I must have done something to make Rex angry with me." I shook my head while listening but remained silent as I thought about how many times I had heard this before.

After any incident that involves a dog attacking a family member, the owner usually takes the blame. Because these owners believe their dog is very much like a human and carries the same emotional and moral qualities as they and their family, they can only reason that the attack was provoked by some action of theirs. After all, what other explanation could there be? The dog had amply demonstrated its love for them for years just like they had for it. Until the attack occurred, they were one, big, happy family. While I was still pondering over this, my client continued. " My son and daughter-in-law are right. If I'm a good grandmother, I'll have to put Rex to sleep because he bit my grandson for no reason." With that, the tears began to well up in her eyes again.

When did we lose our way? As a nation of dog lovers, we have become hopelessly lost. We no longer own dogs for pets; instead, we own make-believe humans in fur coats, and we treat them as such. In our failure to recognize what it is we really own, we have wandered into a fairy tale existence where we believe dogs and humans reason and act out the same. This belief has left us hurt, woefully confused, and without answers when our dogs act out in ways we don't expect.

Sadly, nature never intended it to be this way. From the wild wolf who is perfectly suited for its world, she created a wolf that is perfectly suited for ours. But, like a wonderful gift that has been left unopened, our imaginations have fabricated something inside nature's gift that we humans desire and not what was given. If we would only find the will to open the box, we would discover something far greater. Staring up out of the box would be a domestic wolf born of a rich heritage and carved from the wild. With its behavior wrapped in the trappings of steadfast predictability, this creature would provide us with trustworthy companionship and the tranquility that comes from understanding and accepting it for what it is and not for what we wish it to be. In a paradoxical way, we would actually get what we really desire.

This old woman had lost her way. Because she did not know the wolf in her dog, the only path she could find that would satisfy the ultimatum she had received was one created by misguided humans, and it led to a dead end. Yet, for the sake of her family, she had already taken her first few steps along that path.

I shook my head in conflict. I pitied this woman and her family for their ignorance, but at the same moment, I also marveled at her strength and conviction during this emotional crisis. Staring into her eyes, she reminded me of a time when my mentor and I came across a mortally wounded female wolf lying in the snow many years ago in Alaska. The wolf was a majestic animal with silver-gray fur that was unsettled by the nasty wounds to her head and torso, and as we approached her, she made no attempt to get up; instead, she followed our every move with her unrelinquishing eyes.

"What happened?" I asked. My mentor stood a few paces away with his eyes narrowed as he scanned the snow in all directions. I could tell by the look on his face that he'd heard me, but I had learned quite some time ago that he didn't always answer my questions. Sometimes, he ignored them until I asked them in a way that suited him more. Other times, he would make me answer them myself. However, on those occasions that involved possible danger, he would do what he was doing now, narrow his eyes in total concentration, lock his jaw, and ignore me until he was ready. Taking that as my cue, I unslung my rifle, knelt down, and reflexively went through the steps required to ensure it was ready to fire, all while tracking any sign of possible danger the wild was willing to yield.

"You won't be needing that rifle kid. It's just you, me, and this old she-wolf, and she's in no shape to pose a problem," my mentor said, kneeling next to the wounded wolf whose breath was becoming increasingly more labored. His eyes had changed from their trademark narrow slits to the soft, distant gaze I would see every time his eyes settled on the Brooks Mountain Range, the first snowflakes of the year, the last rays of sun fighting their way through the tops of the spruce trees, or when he closed the door to his cabin to mark the end of another outing into the wild. It was as though he never wanted those moments to end, and through his eyes, he pulled those moments into his heart where they never would. This broken wolf was being tucked away forever. In a silent language that I had yet to learn, she acknowledged my mentor's gesture with a slight lifting of her head, and then she left this world with the same silence and composure that had kept her alive in it.

"She had been displaced by her pack," my mentor explained. *"Most likely too old to have been productive enough to keep around. This was her final attempt to make a kill before she starved to death."* The wolf's death had been the result of a desperate attempt to bring down an adult moose by herself on a bitterly cold February morning. Hundreds of wolf and moose tracks mixed with blood gave an account of the final moments of a life spent in a land where nothing is free and where death is all too often the price that must be paid.

"How could her pack do that to her? It's not right," I pro-
tested angrily.

"*It's not?*" my mentor said as he stood up. His eyes had
changed back to the trademark slits that meant I had better be
careful where I tread with my answer. Even so, I threw caution to the wind because I was angry at the unfairness of it all.
"No sir," I answered.

My mentor did not respond immediately. Instead, he continued to stare at me while his lips formed a smile. I felt my
heart rate start to rise as I knew that particular smile was not
one of approval; rather, it was the same smile a hen saw right
before the fox killed it. My mentor began, "*Nature culls the
weak, old and unproductive, kid. She has to. This ensures there
will be enough food for the young, strong wolves who, unlike the
old, weak wolves, are able to reproduce and make more young,
strong wolves. You don't have to agree with it, kid; you just have
to accept it. Nature is always right.*" Well, I didn't accept it at
that time, and my thoughts must have registered on my face;
as we headed away from the dead wolf, he quietly
added, "*Don't ever grow old, kid; if you do, when you get displaced by a younger society, try to leave this world like that she-
wolf—quietly, but on your feet, fighting to the end.*"

———

My client was no longer a victim. She had determined a plan
of action, and like the mortally wounded wolf, she was determined to face the consequences of her dog's actions without a
whimper and fight to the end. In just a few short moments, she
had transformed from a helpless grandmother to a woman
whom I cared for and admired. I wanted to help her and give

her the knowledge that would spare her dog's life and restore her relationship with her family.

Leaning towards her, I reached out and took her hands in mine. As I looked into eyes that were resolved not to shed another tear, I asked, "Would you like to keep your dog and have your grandson continue to visit you?" At first, there was no answer, only silence. Then, ever so slowly, her hands began to quiver, and her eyes began to blink rapidly. Both gave way to the hope that was cautiously rising in her. Quietly, she asked, "Of course, but how?"

"Come take a journey with me on a path of three prints," I said. "A path that travels through the wild where the wolf lives and through the land where your beloved Rex lives. At the end of the journey, the path will become two prints but remain as three. It is there that you will come to understand why Rex attacked your grandson and why he does so many of his other behaviors. You will also learn how to lead Rex and control him. With this knowledge, you will create the vibrant and stable coexistence that nature intended for both of you, and then your grandson will be welcomed back into your home."

I paused for a moment to let her consider all that I had said, and it was then that I became aware of the strong grip that had replaced her feeble, shaking hands. "A path of three prints that becomes two but remains as three? I'm not sure if I understand what that means, but I'm not afraid to find out. Especially, if it saves Rex's life," she said quietly.

I smiled at my client who had suddenly become like a frightened child holding on for dear life to the hands that she believed would make everything okay again. Ironically, she did not understand, but she had faith, and her faith was all that was needed to understand. Grinning, I explained, "It's a bit of a riddle, one that a very special man taught me when I was a young boy growing up in Alaska. It will make sense to you in the end, and it will bring you peace."

Slowly, my client turned away from me and stared out the window by her chair. The yearning manner in her gaze communicated an enduring loss that time had yet to heal. After a few moments, she softly exhaled and whispered, "My husband was a very special man as well." Then, as she turned back to me, she asked, "Did this man take you on the same journey that you are about to take me?"

Now it was my turn to stare out the window. I had done my best to be the rock that my client could lean on, but the memories of my journey on the path of three prints with my mentor had resurrected my own enduring loss. But, while I watched the top of the pine trees framing the window dance in the wind, I heard a voice from the past. *"Hey, kid. What are you waiting for? You already know all the waypoints for this journey, so plot the course and get moving. The sun sets early this time of year, and it's about to set on this old lady who's counting on you to save her dog. Remember to set a good pace, but don't lose her along the way."*

Even in my memories, my mentor was still a rock I could lean on, and now it was my turn to be the same for my client.

Facing her, I returned her strong grip and answered, "Yes ma'am, he did."

The tears that she had tried so hard to hold back won their way and began to stream down her face. This time, she did not turn away. Instead, she leaned forward to hug me and whispered into my ear, "Lead the way."

What Wolf Is This?

If all the beasts were gone, men would die
from a great loneliness of spirit;
for whatever happens to the beasts
also happens to man.
All things are connected.
Whatever befalls the earth,
befalls the sons of the earth.
~ Chief Seattle

When it comes to dog behavior and the modification of such, there are many theories and methodologies that have been disputed for many years and certainly will be disputed for many more to come. However, with the advances of science, one can no longer argue that today's domestic dog, *canis lupus familiaris,* is a direct descendant of the gray wolf, *canis lupus.* In fact, anyone with an *ist* at the end of their professional title, which includes geneticists, biologists, ethologists, archaeologists, paleontologists, and taxonomists, all agree on this point. They may disagree on the "wheres" and "whens" of it all, but they will all agree that the dog and its wild cousin, the wolf, are more closely related than previously thought. In a 1997 report to the Colorado Task force charged with investigating whether wolf hybrids should be banned in the state, Dr. Ray Pierotti, a geneticist at the University of Kansas; Dr. Nick Federoff, a wildlife biologist; and Dr. Erich Klinghammer, an ethologist from Battleground Indiana Wolf Park, report, "There is no genotype (the genetic constitution of an animal) or phenotype (the observable appearance of an animal) to distinguish between a dog, a wolf-dog cross and a wolf." They then went on to further explain, "There are no known DNA markers uniquely distinguishable in wolves that are not present in dogs."[1]

Years ago, while teaching a dog obedience class, I had a young couple point to their white, fluffy Bichon Frise and comment, "Bryan, I can see the wolf in your German Shepherd, but it's very hard to see the wolf in our dog!" Granted, it may be difficult to see the wolf in a Bichon Frise, but this is due mainly in part to man's attempt to domesticate the wolf for over 120 centuries. In the process, we have created domestic wolves (dogs), whose outside appearances are radically different than that of wolves and are characterized by pointed snouts and ears and lean, athletic torsos supported by legs with large paws that can cover long distances. In contrast, floppy ears and short, blocky snouts with even shorter legs are found in many of today's dog breeds while curled tails, elongated bodies, and outward turned paws are found in others. These physical changes have also radically degraded the performance capability of our domestic wolves. In comparison to the wolf of the wild that can easily cover seventy kilometers per day over rugged terrain and can pull down an animal that outweighs it by hundreds of pounds, today's domestic wolf can barely cover seventy kilometers in a car or pull a comforter off a bed!

We have further complicated our ability to see the wolf in our dogs by our persistent attempts to divert their innate behaviors to what we desire. In the process, we have created domestic wolves that herd and protect sheep instead of chasing and killing them. Domestic wolves fetch ducks, tennis balls, and frisbees and actually give them back to what would have been labeled the "competition" in the wild! These same domestic wolves can be found in our beds and on our laps, on rural farms and in crowded cities. They guide the blind and hear for the deaf. They search for the lost and protect the weak. They give hope to the hopeless and bring healing to the sick. Loyal, dedicated, and above discrimination are common descriptions of our dogs, along with terms of endearment such as "man's best friend."

Some time ago, domestic wolves became as interwoven in the American culture as baseball, apple pie, and the Fourth of July. In most households, the domestic wolf has even trumped evolution itself and jumped straight to being four-legged humans where they are adorned with human names, designer outfits, and fed diets that would confound even the best nutritionist. Is it any wonder why we've granted them our human intelligence and our sacred human emotions as well? Heck no!

Why? They're not dogs; they're family! Yet, for all that nature, time, and man has done to carve the wolf from the wild to create a surrogate human, today's dog is still a wolf at heart, and the accompanying instincts borne from such ancestry define how the dog approaches its world.

Mark Derr, a well-known author and journalist, remarks in his book, *How the Dog Became a Dog: From Wolves to Our Best Friend,* with the following:

> *"That the dog is a wolf modified by nature,*
> *wolves, and humans is as nearly beyond*
> *dispute as an evolutionary line of descent can be.*
> *The domestic dog left unchecked*
> *would be a highly social, tactically minded,*
> *pack-hunting, global wanderer."* 2

This is the reason why most dog owners fail to achieve the control and stability they need or the emotional benefit they so dearly covet from their dogs. They fail to simply accept their dog for what it is: a wolf at heart. Instead, they continue to try to carve their dog from the wild to meet the personal wants or needs that may be lacking in their lives. They may want companionship, or they may need help with a disability or work; either way, what they seek is a "perfect" human and not a domestic wolf. They are blind to the obvious indicators that point to the close relationship our dogs and wolves still share. Like someone staring at an abstract painting, they get lost in the colors and only see what they want to see.

Questions I have asked myself for years are why don't we accept our dogs for what they are and why do we try so desperately to detach them from their wolf heritage when embracing such would allow for a much more successful coexistence?

A lifetime of studying wolves and other social predators along with domestic dogs and their interactions with their human owners has led me to believe there may be several possible reasons:

1. We really don't know very much about wolves and how they relate to our dogs. Sure, we all learn a little about wolves in our high school biology class, but no meaningful comparison is drawn between their behavior and that of our dogs. Also, hindering our knowledge is our inability to compare the two species through personal observation of both wolves and dogs. Most of America's population resides well outside known wolf territories, and the wolves that occupy those territories have no desire to be studied by humans. Add these two factors together, and it's easy to understand our lack of desire to associate our dogs with wolves. It's hard to associate or compare your dog with something you're not familiar with.

2. We have been cleverly persuaded by a multi-billion dollar pet industry that the dog's wolf ancestry is no longer relevant and that it should be cast aside to make way for the new age "human-like" dog that bears no resemblance to its wild cousin and is currently owned by very generously spending human owners.

3. Most Americans are afraid of wolves even though you are more likely to be killed by a dog, a horse or a bee.3 Therefore, why would you want to snuggle up with something you fear, let alone allow your children to play with it?

4. We have become confused by the opinions and recommendations of an ever-growing number of self-proclaimed dog behavioral experts who have never studied wolves in their natural habitat. Their knowledge of wolf behavior is based upon conceptual, not experiential, learning. Therefore, they lack the ability to properly identify the origin or cause of problem behaviors in our dogs and make the correct recommendations to deal with them. This inability on their part would be akin to you trying to figure out how to get to a certain destination without knowing your starting point.

5. We have been led astray by professional dog trainers and veterinarians that have caved to a public sentiment that embraces a positive training only ideology. These trainers and veterinarians suggest that today's dog is so far removed from the wolf that only a loving and nurturing approach to all behavior modification is needed to cultivate a safe and harmonious relationship with them.

6. As a whole, American dog owners lack the "will" to treat their dogs the same as dogs would treat other dogs or wolves would treat other wolves. Wolves don't beg, plead, or negotiate the terms of their conditions, and neither do dogs. However, we do so with our dogs, and like our children, we would rather our dogs obey us because they love us and they want to please us rather than make them do anything.

7. We are being inundated with propaganda from many "no kill" animal shelters and rescue groups that believe there are no unfit dogs, just unfit owners.4 They exploit our fragile

human consciousness in order to obtain our help in saving dogs that are dangerous and unable to safely conform to human companionship. They do this by making us believe that all these dogs need to overcome their condition is the loving relationship of a family.

8. Lastly, we are human and yearn for the companionship and affection of other humans. When that need can't be filled by real humans, a dog is often the acceptable substitute.

In summary, we are not adequately educated in regard to wolves and their behavior, and what little we do know, we are afraid of. So, we turn our backs on nature and her wolf and the direction they are able to provide in achieving a proper existence with our dogs; we seek guidance from a multitude of professionals and organizations that are every bit as unschooled in the ways of wolves and dogs as we are. Disillusioned and frustrated with the volumes of misinformation that are infused into the dog-owning world by these people, we simply turn to what we do know—being human—because making our dogs human makes them easier to love and understand.

In the same basic obedience group class that I mentioned previously in this chapter, I had a student validate my theory. I was talking to another student when I heard from behind me a woman's voice saying, "If you behave and don't embarrass me today, we will stop by Dairy Queen on the way home, and I'll get you an ice cream." Hearing this caused me some concern because I don't allow small children to attend my group classes for safety reasons. Prepared to reiterate this point, I turned around only to find there was no small child—just a young woman with her dog ready to participate in class.

On another occasion, I met with an elderly couple whose dog was causing a bit of marital discord. Having become empty nesters a few years ago, the husband was ready to travel the world and check off a few places on his bucket list. However, his wife of forty-two years would not travel to any destination that required flying because the airlines forbid their large Collie, Leroy, from flying in the passenger cabin with them, and she would not consider boarding him or leaving him with a sitter. When I explained this was standard policy involving non-service dogs, she argued, "I don't understand such a policy. After all, they let other humans that are much bigger than Leroy fly. Trust me! I've had to sit next to them!" Keeping as straight a face as I could at that moment, I rebutted with, "Of course they do; they're humans. Leroy is a dog!" Truly, if looks could kill, I would have died right then. As I took a few steps back to create a safe distance from the woman, she hissed, "Leroy is NOT a dog!" And with that, she turned on her heels and stormed out of the room.

I could easily fill volumes of books with stories similar to these, but hopefully, you get my point. Dogs are great to think of as human. I have owned many dogs in my lifetime, and have I ever treated them like a human? You bet I have. My dogs have been known to taste cheeseburgers, pizza, potato chips, and even an occasional bad-tasting beer! They've sat next to me on the sofa while I watched football games and snuggled up to me on a mountain hillside in the wild. They have been some of the best buddies a guy like me could ask for. Most have passed from my life, but I still miss every one of them. That's what owning a dog is supposed to be. An experience that makes you miss the one that's gone, love the one you have now, and yearn for the one you will have tomorrow.

I can't possibly imagine my life without a dog, and I hope this book grants you the knowledge to have the same feelings. I wrote this book for that purpose. Many years ago, I came to accept dogs for what they are. When I treated them like humans, it was only in pretend and for fun. I never lost sight of the beautiful, individual creation that nature made, and I never disrespected that creation by trying to dress it up as something it wasn't. The dog is a modified wolf, not a human. It is closer in instinct to the wolf than human instinct. It navigates its world through the eyes of a wolf, not a human. The language it speaks and understands is wolf, not human. It will be born as a wolf, live among humans as a dog, and die as a wolf.

One day, as a young man in Alaska, I was harnessing up my dogs in preparation for an amateur mushing event, and I was struggling a bit, as usual, with my lead dog who was always ready to run before I was ready for him to. When I finally got his harness buckled, I was approached by an Alaskan Indian who pointed at my dog and asked, "What wolf is this?" "That's my lead dog, Ranger," I managed to puff out as I moved on to a much easier dog to harness. Ranger was a big, strapping dog that was the envy of many other mushers. With his deep chest, long legs, and unconquerable will, he could motivate even the slowest team to run their fastest or drop dead trying! However, he could be quite the handful right before a race or whenever he wasn't pulling a sled. The Indian stood there staring at Ranger for what seemed a very long time. Then, without taking his eyes off Ranger, he stated, "He's no dog. He's a wolf. Treat him like one, and he will run faster and with more spirit." Hmmm, a wolf? I knew dogs were basically wolves at heart, but before I could get too deep into that thought, the Indian chuckled and said, "You will also get him ready to race faster!"

Six hours later, my team crossed the finish line in second place. While being congratulated by the racing committee and my fellow mushers, the same Indian walked up to me and pointed at my lead dog and asked again, "What wolf is this?" With more than an ounce of pride, I walked over and rested my hand on Ranger's broad head and answered, "This is my lead wolf, Ranger." The Indian turned to me and slowly nodded his head. After a bit, he smiled and stated, "Ranger is a fine wolf."

Ranger and I went on to win a few races over the years. Heeding the Indian's advice, I changed how I handled Ranger and became a bit of a wolf myself in doing so. I allowed him to assert his leadership over the rest of the team, and I did not interfere with any methodology or process he chose. At the same time, I began to assert my leadership over Ranger and, taking my cue from nature, did my best to replicate the same methodology that Ranger used. When I told Ranger it was time to harness up, he began to do so immediately. When Ranger told the rest of the team to run, they ran. Perhaps it was my imagination, but within a few weeks, Ranger and the other dogs did seem to run faster and with even more determination to win. It was as though the spirit of the wild the Indian spoke of had caught fire and was now burning through their fur and through my being. They began to throw all they had into their harnesses, and I howled and yipped along with them as the snow trails blurred under their paws and my sled. We had become a wolf pack in pursuit, and it was so right, so very right.

I would never see that Indian again, but his question became embedded in my heart and still plays off my lips today whenever I meet a new client with their dog. "What wolf is this?" I always ask. I do this because he was right. If we treat our dogs like the wolves they are, they change, and in the process, we change. They run faster and with the spirit of the wild while we are treated to a glimpse of nature's perfection and breathe in the harmonic resonance that runs with the wolf.

"What wolf is your wolf?"

Untruths

An old Cherokee is teaching his grandson about life.
"A fight is going on inside me," he said to the boy.
"It is a terrible fight, and it is between two wolves.
One is evil—he is anger, greed, superiority, lies,
false pride, and ego." He continued, *"The other is good —*
he is love, humility, generosity, empathy, truth,
compassion, and faith. It is going on inside of you —
and inside every other person, too."

The grandson thought about it for a minute
and then asked his grandfather,
"Which wolf will win?"

The old Cherokee simply replied,
"The wolf you feed."

Years ago while shopping in a large, national chain pet store, I was questioned by an employee as to why I had chosen the plastic, enclosed kennel I was carrying to the register instead of the more expensive, all-wire kennel that was most popular. I explained to the employee that my eight-week-old pup would feel more secure in the kennel that I had chosen. The adult wolf is an apex carnivore and does not suffer from natural predation; however, wolf cubs do not share that same secure status and would be very vulnerable to other predators of the forest if not kept safely underground until they grew into enough size to at least eliminate large eagles, hawks, and owls from the list of wolf cub hunters. Because domestic dogs still share many of the same survival instincts as wolves, my pup, like a wolf cub, would feel more protected in the enclosed kennel because of its den-like environment.

After sharing this information with the employee, she promptly lifted her head a little higher, and while wagging a finger at me, she exclaimed, "Sorry, sir, but you have your information all wrong." Really? I have it all wrong? This employee couldn't have been but a few years beyond her pre-pubescent age, and the finger wagging at me looked way too soft to have ever been wagged in subfreezing temperatures while studying wolves in the wild. I couldn't wait to hear her explain to me how I had it all wrong. She reasoned, "Dogs have lived with people for so long that they don't relate to being a wolf anymore. If they have to spend time in a cage, they would rather have a 360-degree view with lots of natural light and fresh air just like you and me. That's why we sell more of the wire cages than the plastic ones."

I could have chosen to lecture her on how *she* had it all wrong by explaining how the 360-degree, panoramic view she loved would have been interpreted by my pup or a wolf cub as, "I can be attacked from any angle." The natural light she adored would have interrupted my pup's, or a wolf cub's, sleeping patterns, and the fresh air would have washed out my pup's, or a wolf cub's, scent which would have been important in identifying its den and would have carried the alien and threatening scent of the large dogs that belonged to my neighbor next door. I could have further explained the obvious in that dogs are not human, and therefore, to assume they desired what she desired had no scientific backing to support it and was a far-fetched conjecture and wishful thinking on its best day. Instead, I simply asked her where she had obtained her knowledge on the subject; she responded with "on the Internet." With that, I nodded, thanked her for her assistance, and took up my place in the checkout line with my enclosed plastic kennel held firmly in my hand.

The majority of the human population does not dwell in the interior of Alaska or any known geographical area inhabited by gray wolves, leaving most people the inability to lay eyes on a free wolf in their lifetimes. These people live in heavily populated, urban cities and dream of getting away to those remote areas. However, life simply won't allow it as school, careers, and child-rearing takes precedence over expensive trips to the wild where the chances of actually seeing an elusive wolf are more remote than the landscape they occupy. Real life opportunities to observe wolf behavior becomes minimal at best, leaving exposure to wolves, and more importantly their behavior, to books, movies, the Internet, and advertisements.

Sadly, the authors of most of these sources have never spent a second in the wild observing wolves, leaving us to question the reliability of their information. These individuals can acquire an immense, conceptual knowledge of wolves, somewhat inconsistent, from all the material available today and pass it on to the world. However, to accurately represent the wolf, you would need the assistance of experiential knowledge to validate any conceptual understanding. To gain this experiential knowledge, you would have to immerse yourself in the world of the wolf. Think of it like reading several books on climbing Mount Everest. By doing so, you would become familiar with terms such as crampons, belaying, fissures, and so forth, but to gain real knowledge of what it's like to climb the mountain, you would have to strap on those crampons, belay your line, avoid deep fissures, and head for the summit. If you manage to make it to the top and back down again in one piece, you would become a firm believer in that experiential knowledge trumps conceptual knowledge every day of the week!

Because of the lack of experiential know-how associated with wolf behavior and the effect this has had on the reliability of the information made available, unenlightened dog owners are left to sift through a myriad of truths and untruths surrounding the wolf-dog relationship and its relevance. Such misinformation is often the product of a collective ignorance or a willful disregard for what is true. That today's dog is a direct descendant of the gray wolf and its behaviors originated from and are dominated by that phylogenetic relationship is the truth. That today's dog is so far removed from the wolf in the evolutionary process that its behavior has become more influenced by the humans that love it is the untruth.

The truth is a very difficult pill to swallow for most dog lovers. After all, it is way more fun to think of your dog as a little person in a fur coat, and it certainly makes it easier to explain away why your dog bit you when you tried to take your shoe out of its mouth. I remember such a case when a client, while showing me her bandaged right hand, explained why she was the recipient of a nasty bite when she tried to remove one of her favorite boots from her beloved dog who had a very solid grip on the expensive leather. "He wasn't being mean; he just didn't like me wearing those boots! He was trying to tell me they didn't look good on me." Funny as this seems, when we think our dogs think like this, reality and all of her wisdom and comfort walk out the door, and trouble and instability walk in.

So, who's responsible for the genesis of these untruths that has led to the deterioration of the human-to-dog relationship? Ultimately, it is the unsuspecting pet owner who lavishly spends money in the pursuit of dog ownership nirvana. They swallow anything published, produced, or peddled that guarantees a paradisiacal relationship with their best friend, and then they are left dazed, confused, and abandoned when the anthropomorphic honeymoon ends and the wolf sets in. I have listened to the stories of thousands of dog owners when this moment occurs, and, like a deer caught in headlights, they never see it coming. As you are reading this book, is this happening to you right now? If it is, before you choke on this revelation, you need to understand you had a lot of help arriving at this moment, sixty billion dollars a year worth of help!

The pet industry in America is a robust, multi-billion dollar game of emotional influence that has never suffered from an economic decline. It employs a business model cleverly designed to separate you from your hard-earned dollar, and to keep that separation happening at record levels, they need to keep separating you from the truth. Discrimination of social-economic status does not factor into limiting the players in this game either. An article reported in the *U.S. News and World Report*, May 22, 2013, declares: "It turns out even the deepest recession in decades can't kill off pet spending. The average household spends greater than $500 per year on each pet. *The Labor Department* reports 'Americans remained self-lessly devoted to their pets during the recession, holding their spending on pet food steady through the downturn while cutting back on the luxury of eating out.' " 5

Corporations that produce the essentials for dog ownership such as pharmaceuticals, food, and treats, along with beds, cages, and training equipment are the biggest winners while veterinarians, groomers, and dog trainers clean up what's left over. Everyone wants a piece of the economic pie, and the crust that holds the filling is not made of the correct notion that you own a domestic wolf but rather by anthropomorphism and its all-powerful pull on the human heart.

According to *The U.S. Trade Group*, March 2013, "All this suggests a bright future for an industry that has grown alongside the popularity of pets, expanding at a steady four percent to six percent a year since the American Pet Products Association started record-keeping in 1996. What is feeding a large part of the growth now are the baby boomers who have become empty-nesters and are looking for some other way to find the love and affection they used to get from their kids." In the same article, Dr. Jessica Vogelsand, a San Diego veterinarian, explains, "In the past, children were a reflection of us, and people are now extending that to their pets." 6

As our life spans increase, the likelihood that we will find ourselves living alone without the constant companionship of our children or our spouse does, too. Owning a dog helps to fill the emotional void created by our loneliness. With a dog, you have someone to talk to, to care for, and to snuggle with in bed. Most of all, you have someone who makes you leave the confines of your home, and because 56.7 million other American dog owners are also leaving the confines of their homes, there is a greater probability you will encounter one of them and perhaps strike up a friendship or even find yourself in a new relationship.

A great deal of money has been invested by the pet industry to tap into the human psyche and influence our current perception of the dog as a little person in a fur coat. They have nurtured our loneliness and longing for a surrogate human and turned it into billions of dollars. Like watching a magician who makes use of a slick illusion to distract us from what's really happening, we have been made to believe our dogs possess special human traits that are needed to combat our human loneliness and achieve a perfect family. We are then subjected to one "happy dog complementing the perfect, happy family" advertisement after another. A smiling dog along with a smiling human adorns the vast majority of the products available, while movies depict dogs having a greater ability of deduction than the actors playing alongside them. In recent years, dog training that employs "positive reinforcement only" has gained popularity because the use of any "wolflike" force in establishing reliable behaviors has been deemed cruel and inhumane by those trainers who advocate its use. I recently interviewed such a trainer, and as I listened to her passionately defending her all-positive methodology, I couldn't help but notice the slogan stenciled on the treat bag hanging from her hip. It read, "Keep calm and treat." Good to keep that in mind the next time we try using just treats alone to persuade our dogs to come back to us rather than pursue a squirrel racing across a busy highway. No wonder avoiding uncontrolled animals is one of the top twenty-five causes of automobile accidents in the United States!

If a clever business model making use of slick illusions wasn't enough to empty our wallets and lead us astray, the pet industry also profits from our natural fear of wolves. Research has shown that wolves top the list of animals most feared by Americans, although we have a far greater chance of being killed by a bee, a horse, or even our own dog. Entrepreneurial strategists utilize this information to support their anthropo-morphous campaigns and discredit any studies that attest to the similarities of dog and wolf behavior. They know, all too well, that if we ever came to embrace a domestic wolf instead of the substitute human they have convinced us we own, then our spending would decrease dramatically as we became more practical and began to forgo purchasing half of the gimmicks currently produced. Those items would no longer be of value in our new and improved relationship with our dogs.

The ontogeny of anthropomorphism in our pets is, by far, the most damaging and paralytic problem associated with dog ownership today. Believing in a fairy tale world where dogs possess the same moral consciousness and sense of altruism as attributed to humans only leads us down the path of untruths where consequences await. Big business is aware of these consequences, but you won't find them listed on any dog food bags or on any bolstered dog beds. It's a numbers game to them, and like Las Vegas, the house wins. Their profits rise every year at about the same level as reported dog bites requiring medical attention do. They get rich while you're left holding the bill with a bandaged hand.

A marketing agent from a dog treat manufacturing company approached me a few years ago in the hope of soliciting my endorsement of their product. The product was a new, organic, gluten- and sugar-free treat for dogs. The agent claimed that disobedience on the part of our dogs was to be blamed on the multitude of poor quality treats available on the market that had caused our dogs' energy levels to reach a nervous, hyper-metabolic state that resembled ADHD in children. A sudden decrease in the ability to focus after consuming several of the poor quality treats had left most dogs with the inability to understand their owner's commands. The agent then summarized his sales pitch by stating that the use of their product during training would have the opposite effect on dogs by actually increasing their ability to focus on commands. This, of course, would then lead to better behaved dogs and happier dog owners.

What was more remarkable than his absurd claim was the fact that he actually believed it! An organic, gluten- and sugar-free dog treat was to be the savior of American dog owners with problematic dogs. *Simply dangle the organic treat in front of your dog's nose, and every wish of yours will be obeyed immediately with joy and an indefatigable focus.* When I countered with the suggestion that if we tried putting our foot in our problematic dog's butt every now and then, we would achieve a much higher rate of reliability and focus than any treat would, regardless of its ingredients, I thought he was going to have a stroke.

I have never trusted big, corporate businesses to lead me correctly in regard to understanding dogs or solving their problem behaviors. Instead, I have always placed my trust in nature. Mankind has been straying from the path of righteousness since Adam, whereas nature's compass has always held to true north. Over the years, I have been heedful of her unrelenting will to hold fast to the natural instincts she infused in her wolves and passed to our dogs.

The pet industry intentionally diverts our attention away from the wolf in our dogs all while producing one gimmick after another that promises a relationship with our dogs that only treating them like a wolf will provide. What pet industries fail to understand is that if we simply "make" our dogs obey us, like wolves make wolves obey, we would not need to rely upon their magical treats or the other nonsense they produce. In doing so, we would achieve the connection with our dogs that only nature's lesson plan can provide. Because their instincts were cast in the same primordial mold as wolves, we can always rely upon nature's guidance to steer us through the seemingly complex behaviors of today's domestic dogs instead of big business.

My personal dogs have never needed a leash to control them. Their responses to my cues have always been unfailingly reliable because I have always trained them according to nature's plan. I did not deviate from this plan when I was introduced to the latest and greatest fad in training or when I was asked to endorse the latest and greatest product or equipment. Instead, I held steadfast to nature's course, and as a result, the quality of life I have enjoyed with my dogs is immeasurable. There is no better joy for a dog owner than to see his dog looking at him like he means something, like he's an irreplaceable part of his life and like he's supposed to be obeyed. And there is no better joy for a dog than to be treated and respected by his owner for what he really is and not for what he really isn't. Like the wolf, he is supposed to run swiftly and freely and give way to his leader's direction. It is as nature intended.

––––––––––

"What are you making there, kid?" I about stab myself with my knife at the suddenness of my mentor's voice. Like usual, I failed to hear him walk up on me.

"I'm making a new type of trap for snowshoe hares," I answer and then lift up the small box with a spring-loaded door that I have been working on all afternoon so he can see it.

"Hand it here. I want to take a closer look at it." With pride, I hand over my new creation for my mentor to admire.

My trap looks small in his big hands as he turns it over and inspects every square inch of it. *"How's it supposed to trap a hare?"* he asks.

This is getting better by the second! Not only is he admiring my trap, but now, my great and powerful mentor is asking me to explain how it works! I can't believe it. Just when I thought he knew everything about everything, I suddenly discover he doesn't! Excitedly, I go on to explain how, according to the most recent *Sports Afield* magazine I had just read, when a hare enters the open end of the box to nibble on the succulent blueberry leaves that the trap will be baited with, the hare will brush up against a carefully concealed trip wire that will release the spring-loaded door, and bingo, the hare will be trapped!

"Sorry you wasted your time making this trap, kid," my mentor remarks as he hands back my trap. He adds, *"No snowshoe hare I know of is gonna go in that box no matter what you put in it, succulent blueberry leaves or not."*

I'm stunned. Never did I see this as the outcome of my hard, diligent, four hours of work. My temporarily inflated ego has just been popped by my great and powerful mentor once again. *When will I ever learn?* I think to myself. "But according to *Sports Afield*, this trap will work," I rebut. "When I camouflage it, a hare won't know it's a box. He'll just think he's stumbled across a great snack in the middle of the brush."

"I don't know much about what Sports Afield *knows, but I do know quite a bit about snowshoe hares that live in the Alaskan wild. Perhaps the gentleman that wrote about that trap of yours in* Sports Afield *can use that box to catch a hare in the Lower 48, but you ain't gonna catch an Alaskan hare with one of those."* To add salt to my already wounded ego, my mentor starts to chuckle.

"Why not?" I ask angrily. In my mind, I can see a hare going in my trap all day long!

"Camouflage it all you want, kid, but the hares we hunt will know it's a box, and they won't go in it. Like I said, in the Lower 48, they may because they've been known to make burrows down there where the ground ain't frozen year round. However, up here, it is; therefore, they'll just make a shallow depression under thick brush to hide from wolves and other predators until nightfall when they come out from under that brush to eat. The shallow depression they make provides for concealment, but, push come to shove with a predator, that hare

can light out in any direction it needs to escape. That's why you won't catch one going in something like your box that only allows one direction for escape. Once again, kid, sorry you wasted a good afternoon on that box, but man can't influence a wild Alaskan hare to change its behavior and go in it; only nature can."

With that, he concludes our debate by turning and walking away. I'm not sure if it was the stubbornness or the ignorance of my youth, but I tried out my trap anyway for the next few months, and of course, I never caught a hare. Nature always wins, and this time, my mentor let me teach the lesson to myself.

When you finish reading this chapter, set this book down, turn off your TV, silence your smartphone, and just spend a few minutes observing your dog. If you watch, nature will show you the wolf in your dog. If you listen, nature will tell you about the wolf in your dog. If you trust her, nature will guide you to the wolf in your dog. Look for it because it's there. Do not fear the wolf you discover because if nature did not intend for it to be there, it would not be. No matter how hard the pet industry tries to make this wolf vanish with all of their well-contrived misrepresentations, it will always be there. Your acceptance of this truth and not the untruths of the pet industry will be necessary for you to take your first step on the path of owning the dog you always dreamed of.

This is the whole truth.

Nothing to Fear

If you talk to the wolves, they will
talk with you, and you will know each other.

If you do not talk to them, you will not know them,
and what you do not know you will fear.
What one fears, one destroys.
~ Chief Dan George

I remember sitting on the hearth of our fireplace as a young boy in Fairbanks, Alaska, during an unusually cold winter evening reading the story of "Little Red Riding Hood." Our home was surrounded by a nearly impassable forest of black spruce and birch, and on occasion while reading, I caught myself stealing a nervous glance out the window to see if there were any wicked wolves lurking behind the tall, dark trees. Funny, I thought, my mentor had seen many wolves in that forest before, and he wasn't afraid of them; the wicked wolf of Little Red Riding Hood also only seemed to be interested in eating grandmothers and little girls, and I was, after all, a boy. So, what was there to be afraid of? Yet, the hair on the back of my neck was standing up like the hackles on our sled dogs when I came to the part where the wicked wolf swallowed grandma. I could feel my heart racing in my chest as I read faster and faster to such a point that I wondered if my pounding heart would end before the story did! But alas, the mighty woodsman came to dispense of the wicked wolf and save the day; mercifully for me, the story came to an end. One day, I thought, as I set down the book, I, too, am going to be a mighty woodsman and master the wolves of the wood.

I was no ordinary kid while growing up in the interior of Alaska. When other kids wished to play baseball in the summer or hockey in the winter, I always wanted to be in the forest. When they were reading comic books, I was reading *Call of the Wild* and *White Fang*. When they were building model airplanes and cars, I was making snowshoes and frames for my pack. I was a creature of the wild, and it was within her embrace that I felt most at home.

Under the skillful guidance of my mentor, I became a woodsman, and I was afforded the opportunity to observe wolves in their natural setting where I learned to master any fear I had of them. My initial imprinting of a "wicked" creature was reset by nature herself when she revealed that the wolf was an intelligent and adaptable predator that could be ruthless and opportunistic when trying to survive, especially in an unforgiving landscape such as where I lived. It was not the creation of fairy tales that employed premeditated evil to obtain its goals. In other words, wolves did not plot to swallow grandmas and little girls whole.

Most American children are not able to benefit from nature's lessons to help them overcome their youthful imprinting of the wolf as a villain like I did. When they read "Little Red Riding Hood," "The Three Little Pigs," or the fairy tales of Brothers Grimm, they close their books and go to their beds where they hide underneath their covers in the hope that the Big Bad Wolf won't find them. These children wake up in the morning in their urban homes void of the ability to cleave the valuable teachings from nature that would contradict their newfound fearful impression of wolves. As they age, they come into contact with even more reinforcers of their fear. In Aesop's fables, they learn of an evil, unforgiving wolf that kills a young, naive lamb. Reading Shakespeare, they learn of pitfalls when trusting wolves. Jesus warns not to behave like a wolf when dealing with others; he uses the wolf as a metaphor in the Bible to describe evil and destructiveness. Three verses in the Quran speak of the wolf as a creature that would surely devour Yusuf. In European folklore, children learn of humans who can shape-shift into the form of a wolf and become a terrifying creature known as a werewolf; in movies such as *The Grey*, they are exposed to Hollywood's depiction of the wolf as a cunning and relentless killer of innocent survivors of a plane crash that occurs in the remote Alaskan wilderness. Is it any wonder why we fear wolves? By the time most people reach adulthood, they've had the Big Bad Wolf crammed down their throats from every conceivable angle! They become convinced the wolf is always the bad guy.

Fortunately for me, living on the Alaskan frontier created a healthy respect for wolves instead of one of fear; as a result, my observations of wolves became more bold, more curious, and more frequent all at the same time. Every opportunity I got, I set out into the wild to look for signs of wolves. I would study their prints to determine where they had come from or where they were going. I would dig in their scat to learn what they had eaten, and like a detective, I would cautiously examine the remains of a large herbivore or ungulate to determine if its fate had been decided by wolves; if I concluded it had, I would then search for clues that would explain the "whens" and "hows" of its death. On rare occasions, I was blessed with actually seeing wolves at a distance through powerful binoculars. I would watch them criss-cross the landscape, sometimes by themselves or in a small group, hunting for that ever-elusive next meal. At times, I would see them running so fast they were but an apparition that flitted among the trees. Engaging in a game of tug-of-war over a branch with the victor playing keep away was a favorite activity among the younger wolves while intermittent fighting could be seen and heard among the adults. Fear had been replaced by a longing for knowledge, and I couldn't get enough.

Months before I had learned from my mentor that dogs were wolves at heart, I was trudging through the melting snow on a mild, spring day looking for wolf signs when a thought came to me. It had been there for quite some time – a consistent prodding of something begging to be discovered that I hadn't been able to find yet because it was hiding in the wide open. For months, I had looked past it while it was under my nose the entire time. And then it hit me as clear as the earth in the vanishing winter landscape on which I was standing. These wolves of the wild that I had been tracking, observing, and studying were uncannily similar to my dogs – not just in the physical sense where both had pointed ears and snouts and lean compact bodies with long legs, but in the behavioral sense as well.

Giving this some thought, I realized my dogs devoured their food like wolves, slept like wolves, and even hunted like wolves. If any of my dogs ever caught a glimpse of a rabbit, they would chase it every bit as vigorously as a wolf would and then later return home where, much to my mother's disapproval, they would deposit their prize at the foot of our back door! They played tug-of-war and keep-away, and they certainly had their share of battles in their attempt to maintain a hierarchy like wolves. In fact, Ranger, who was three years old at the time, the alpha leader of our pack, and my lead sled dog, was challenged for his position by a few of our upcoming young males from time to time. Unfortunately for them, all were quickly thrashed and sent away howling to lick their wounds and rethink why they had attempted such a foolish undertaking. Ranger remained the dominant leader of our pack until the day he died at the age of ten. His reign held steadfast for all of those years by his indomitable presence. Like the alpha wolf of the wild, Ranger's will was always law.

In all of the years I observed wolves in Alaska, I simply could not recall a single behavior common to wolves that was not common to my dogs. I came to realize that at the most primitive level, our dogs still operated like wolves, and their approach to their world was dominated by a powerful instinct graciously given by nature and not by man. This awareness created a deep understanding of how the natural behavior of a species affects the natural behavior of its descendants. Nature has always been the master teacher, and although her fees are often high, she keeps her lessons simple – to the point and with an everlasting consistency. It was as straightforward as that, and I learned all of this without having taken my first real biology class in school.

I grew up feeling like Christopher Columbus in that my explorations had discovered something real and credible that would forever affect my relationship with dogs and those of the people I would come to teach. Like other kids, I went on to read tales by Aesop and the Brothers Grimm. I listened to sermons about Jesus and his use of the wolf as a metaphor, and, only because it was required in school, I read the part in Shakespeare's "King Lear" about not trusting wolves. I watched more than a few movies about werewolves and other creatures like vampires, but I no longer hid underneath my covers afterwards or stole nervous glances out our window. I wasn't afraid of the wolf anymore. He was no longer the Big Bad Wolf I had known when I was younger. Instead, he had inexplicably become something I personally needed.

"Do you see that big male staring at us?" my mentor says as he points at a small group of four wolves standing high on a rock strewn ridge about sixty meters away. Most of them are difficult to make out because their gray and black coats blend so well with the natural colors of the stone and the many Birch and Western Hemlock trees in the background, but one is standing in the open. He is a very large, charcoal gray male with piercing, amber eyes that I am convinced are staring right

at me. Too stunned and frightened to answer, I only nod my head and slowly move closer to my mentor.

"*What's wrong, kid? Does my big friend up there scare you?*" my mentor chuckles as he places a reassuring arm around my shoulders. This is only my fourth outing into the wild with him and my first to actually see wolves up close. I had seen wolves one other time before, but they had been so far away, I'd had to borrow my mentor's binoculars just to say I had seen them. "Kinda," I whisper sheepishly. This may only be my fourth trip with my mentor, but I have already learned he isn't afraid of anything, and he despises anyone who is.

He continues, "*Well, there's nothing to fear. That big fella and I became acquainted about a year back. At that time, I was running a trap line I had laid a few days earlier when I spotted him for the first time. When he caught sight of me, I smiled and stared back. Neither of us moved for a long time, and when we both finally did, neither of us held a trace of fear for each other. He had accepted me, and I had accepted him. This acceptance is everything son. Granted, he's a big wolf and certainly can be dangerous, but nevertheless, he is a wolf, and he has every right to these woods as I do. In his eyes, I'm sure I can be dangerous, too, but he isn't afraid of me because I accept him and do not fear him. Acceptance is trust, kid. Me and old fire eyes trust one another.*" Fire is right. I can almost feel my face scorching from the wolf's intense scrutiny of what I am still convinced is me! Trust or no trust, I can't bear to match the big wolf's stare any longer; embarrassed, I bend over and start adjusting the straps on my snowshoes.

"*What's more important than your snowshoes right now is my big friend up there accepting you like he accepted me, and he's not going to do that if you act afraid of him,*" my mentor added. So much for my snowshoe ploy. I was quickly learning my mentor didn't miss a thing. Reaching over and firmly lifting my chin with his hand, my mentor whispers, *"Look at him and do not look down again. Tell him with your eyes that you are neither an opponent or a threat. Tell him that this forest is your home as well as his and that you accept him in it."*

Accept him? Just because my mentor accepts him doesn't mean I do! This is the wicked wolf of the wood in the flesh, and I just want to be as far away from him as possible. *"Do it now,"* my mentor commands. *"Look him in the eyes and do not look away until I say so."* This doesn't come as a gentle whisper; rather, it comes like the hiss of a snake. I do as I am instructed and slowly lift my eyes from my snowshoes and follow the rocky slope as it bends up to the ridge to where the big wolf is still standing. Before my eyes reach him, I feel his menacing gaze on me, and it's all I can do not to look back down at my snowshoes again. *"Look him in the eyes, kid,"* my mentor hisses, and I fight back the tears that threaten to degrade me further. I am in a pickle: do I disobey my mentor and die for sure or stare the wicked wolf in the eyes and get eaten for sure. What had started out as an adventurous trip into the wild was fast becoming my last trip because I am certain that either path I choose will result in my becoming a goner. With that, I decide I would rather be eaten by this wolf than disappoint the man who is fast becoming my hero and my best friend. I raise my gaze a few more feet, and to my surprise, the big wolf's eyes have changed. They are still fiery embers that continue to burn, but they are not burning in a menacing way anymore. I am still afraid but not as afraid as I was. I find myself staring no longer into the eyes of a wicked wolf created by man's imagination but real eyes that convey an immemorial nobility ordained by nature herself. This is an Alpha wolf, the King of his pack, and the very forest my mentor and I tread; I suddenly feel very small and insignificant in comparison.

"He's something, ain't he, kid?" My mentor's voice seems miles away as I remain transfixed. Moments before, I couldn't bring myself to look at this wolf, and now I can't tear my eyes away. There is a message in his eyes. I am not sure what it is, but I feel accepted by this wolf, and I am no longer afraid. "Yes sir, he is something indeed."

———————

Today, many decades later, I know the message the big wolf was trying to pass along. Perhaps it wasn't meant to be known until now. Perhaps my years of experience or the wisdom gained from a lifetime spent among wolves and dogs was needed to unlock its secret, but I now know what I saw in his eyes, and I am comforted by the simplicity of it all.

Closing my eyes, I travel back to that time, and I feel my mentor's steady hand on my shoulder as I am pulled into the wolf with the fiery eyes where the message awaits. There, I see life with the beginning of all things and death with its unavoidable finality. I see unsullied perfection created and framed by evolution with superiority as a means and subjection as a design. I see courage and resolve where fear and pity reign. I see the resiliency of a primordial instinct that will never yield to man's incessant manipulation. I see a wolf, and he is Ranger. I see my mentor, and he is me. Lastly, I see acceptance, without judgement, of a young boy with fear in his eyes who is ignorant of it all.

Know the Parts

In the beginning of all things, wisdom and knowledge
were with the animals. Tirawa, the One Above,
did not speak directly to man. He sent
certain animals to tell men
that he showed himself through the beast.
From them and from the stars and the sun
and moon should man learn...
all things tell of Tirawa.
~ Eagle Chief (Letakos-Lesa) Pawnee

Owning a dog today comes with its own, customized challenges. Common problems such as housebreaking, chewing on your personal belongings, jumping on you, pulling you down the street, not coming to you when called, and many other agonizing behaviors can make you second guess why you got your dog in the first place! Everywhere you turn for advice, including your family, friends, veterinarians, professional dog trainers, and the Internet, you are met with differing opinions on how best to eliminate these undesirable behaviors. Whom then do you trust? Most dog owners have struggled with this question after both their money and their emotions were drained as they attempted one misguided program after another with no success. Sadly, this siphoning of money and emotions worsens with each passing day as dog owners continue to present their problems to professionals who don't know all of the parts.

Professional dog training, as an occupation, has no federal or statewide accreditations and no national oversight committee to govern its conduct or to control the vast amount of information that is doled out by its practitioners. Anyone who thinks he or she can train a dog can print business cards, develop a website, and label themselves a professional. There is no formal education, certification, or residency requirements, and to make matters worse, there are no required background checks! The professional trainer you just invited into the privacy of your home could be a convicted felon. I guarantee you will not see their rap sheet included with their credentials.

Even those trainers who have paid thousands of dollars to a professional dog trainer's academy in the pursuit of a formal education are often not equipped upon graduation to deal with the widespread challenges that a career in professional dog training provides. To successfully meet these challenges, a graduate would need, at a minimum, a fundamental grasp of canine evolution, genetics, behavior, mechanisms associated with aggression, and the proper methodology to achieve a reliable response to given cues. Other requirements would include a rudimentary understanding of human behavior coupled with the role it plays in influencing canine behavior and the use of psychotropic medications in achieving a manageable state in clinically maladaptive dogs. On top of this, the graduate would have to possess the capability to accurately convey this information to his or her clients and then teach them the necessary skills to achieve their goals.

To date, I have interviewed many graduates from these schools, and not one of them was able to meet these minimum requirements in my opinion. However, their prospective schools still sent them out their doors adorned with impressive titles such as *Master Trainer, Canine Behavioral Modification Expert, Therapy Dog Trainer*, and the like, all while glossing over their woefully inept knowledge and skill set. Recently, my wife and I conducted a working interview with two of the top graduates of a professional dog trainer's academy. The graduates were given a few untrained dogs and asked to demonstrate the skills they had acquired during their six months of instruction. After the interview, we asked a member of our training staff what she thought of the graduates' performances. The staff member replied, "They looked like our clients."

While some trainers feel the need to attend a professional dog trainer's academy, others don't. Instead, they rely upon and boast of diversified degrees in psychology, sociology, and veterinary medicine, and they are willing to put them to use in order to solve any intrusion your dog may be making in your peaceful world. They will call upon instrumental and classical conditioning, throw out names such as Pavlov, Skinner, and Lorenz, and use terms such as object choice tasking, positive and aversive stimuli, and shaping. However, unless they also throw out terms such as naturalistic observation, evolutionary strategy, social awareness, and aggressive mechanisms, their ability to solve dog problems beyond basic dog obedience will be seriously degraded as their approach will only be two dimensional, and that simply doesn't work. Solving dog problems requires a three-dimensional approach: the dog, the humans involved, AND the wolf.

It is not my intent to shed poor light on professional dog trainers or professional training academies as a whole. After all, I am one, and I graduated from one. There are thousands of very talented trainers who are working at the grass roots level every day and making a favorable impact on dog ownership in America. However, it is my intent to point out the flaws in the system. A late friend of mine, who was a real life Japanese sage, once told me, *"When an archer misses the mark, he looks within himself for error; he should remember that four of his fingers are pointing at himself."*

Self-criticism is always the hardest criticism to give, and when you think you know more than the next guy, it's even harder. I have had clients who were top professors at major universities and had been bestowed with more than a few doctorate degrees in their fields of study. They threw out words so big that I needed the use of Wikipedia just to interpret their questions! Some of my clients had been top graduates at service academies and had achieved the rank of General or Admiral in their respective branches of the U.S. Military. I have had rock stars and professional athletes as clients, and others have included doctors, lawyers, and heads of large corporations. I have had some very impressive clients in my day, and some have gotten more knowledge in their fields than I will ever obtain in my lifetime. But, you know what they all had in common? They didn't know squat about dog behavior! That's right, nothing.

So, it doesn't take long, after solving the problems for a few of these types of clients, for a bit of arrogance to set in. When that happens, arrogance takes the front burner and sends self-criticism to the back burner while professional growth is shoved in the oven. If it sounds like I'm confessing, it's because I am. I had fallen prey to my own legend, and my clients and their dogs suffered for it. It took a young girl receiving a serious bite due to my poor judgment before the gravity of self-criticism and its need set in.

There has never been a more pressing time for our profession to take a look at itself and make sure we are acting responsibly. With millions of dogs taking up residence in millions of households across the globe, there will always be millions of behavioral issues that will need the assistance of those who wear the title of a professional dog trainer. It is an unprecedented time in which our dogs are as important to us as our human family. We dog owners will do all that we can to make living with our dogs a success. Professionals in the dog behavior world carry an incredible responsibility as their recommendations will always have a direct effect on that success or failure. These professionals must understand that their inability to give proper advice to dog owners can lead to much more than a dog becoming a brat and taking over the family. It can lead to the dog being rehomed, abandoned, or even euthanized. It can also lead to a child, an adult, or another dog being attacked and suffering a severe injury.

In my thirty years of involvement in the dog behavioral world, I have witnessed the aftermath of improper recommendations given by unqualified trainers. I have seen marriages and families torn apart, children disfigured, dogs killed as scapegoats, and the life savings of dog owners paid to personal injury attorneys. Most of these could have been avoided if a reasonable and logical solution had been presented to the client, one that nature would have provided had the trainer simply looked in her direction. Sadly, thousands of today's dog owners are being misled by professional trainers who are operating in the blind and are caught unaware until they step off a cliff.

Not considering the effect of wolf instinct when dealing with domestic dog problems, whether because of ignorance or a willful disregard, is the major reason why the dog training industry is not achieving the success rate that it should. Most proclaimed training experts have never witnessed a wolf's behavior in the wild, and because most dog behavior can be traced back to the wolf, they are not able to draw a much needed comparison between the two when solving problems. Their lack of both the conceptual and experiential knowledge of wolf behavior, as discussed in Chapter 3, forces them to approach dog behaviors from a humanistic standpoint or rely heavily upon information passed down by their instructors or other trainers whose methodologies are bankrupt for the same reasons. Any expert or trainer who addresses any canine behavioral problem with strictly a humanistic approach is wrong. However, you don't need me telling you that because eventually, if you keep taking their advice, your dog will. Your dog did not come from a human womb; it came from that of a wolf, and if push comes to shove, your dog will convince you of that.

Adding to the problem with professional dog training is the pressure that is coming from a growing anthropomorphic dog-owning society that refuses to allow Fluffy to be subjected to any methodology that incorporates a correction like a wolf. At the slightest suggestion of such, these owners recoil in horror. While cradling Fluffy in their arms, they make it perfectly clear they will not stand by and allow Fluffy's spirit to be broken.

Most professional trainers cave to this pressure because, again, their lack of knowledge associated with wolf behavior leaves them unable to present the reasonable and logical argument that nature makes available. They have never witnessed a wolf correcting the undesirable behavior in another wolf and then observed how that wolf immediately and reliably adjusts its behavior so as not to be corrected again by the very same wolf for the very same offense. They also would have failed to take notice of how the corrected wolf did not sulk afterwards with the "broken spirit" that their anthropomorphic client suggests would occur.

The famous poet, D.H. Lawrence, very accurately penned these sentiments with the following poem:

"I never saw a wild thing sorry for itself.
A small bird will drop frozen dead from a bough
without ever having felt sorry for itself." 7

In nature, day-to-day survival does not allow for the luxury of self-pity, hurt feelings, and grudges like those harbored by humans. A man can have his feelings hurt by his insensitive wife and then become very angry with her. If she fails to apologize for hurting his feelings, he may develop a grudge against her. He may even find himself plotting a just revenge. While this is occurring, he could also drive to a fast food restaurant and get something to eat without his wife's assistance.

The corrected wolf will not harbor any ill feelings toward the correcting wolf. Instead, it will simply adjust its behavior to the input received from the other wolf and move on with life in the pack. While doing so, it will remain as a *vibrant* contributor to the success of the correcting wolf and the pack as a whole. At the end of the day, whether they happen to like each other or not, both wolves need each other for survival. There is no such thing as a "broken spirit" in the wild.

Millions of dogs that are required to be "spot-on" reliable in the performance of duties for the safety of human beings receive "wolf-like" corrections as part of their training. When I was a police K9 officer, my dog Jagr, a Belgian Malinois, was trained using this methodology. During his short, three-year career with me, he saved my life on two occasions, apprehended over fifty criminals, and tracked down an eighty-year-old woman suffering from Alzheimer's disease who had wandered out of her home at one in the morning and in subfreezing temperatures. Doctors say she would have died if Jagr had failed to find her when he did. Jagr was my partner, and I needed 100 percent from him every time I clocked in for duty. Jagr granted me that every night and never once demonstrated anything remotely like a "broken spirit." Instead, he demonstrated the courage, vitality, selflessness, and dedication of the wolf that resided in his heart.

As I continue to explain throughout this book, our dog's behavior is dominated by that thing passed down from the wolf that you can't see under a microscope: instinct. I use the word *dominated* because even though we can use our influence to train a dog to do a behavior, we didn't create it; nature did. For example, you can train your dog to sit, but your dog would sit on its own if not trained by you. Sitting is a transitory position wolves take before they lie down, partly because of mechanical reasons and partly because of the possibility of hazards where they intend to lie down. You can also train your dog to lie down, but your dog would lie down on its own if not trained by you. Wolves lie down when there is nothing productive to do. Nature punishes excessive energy use, so lying around helps conserve valuable calories.

In order to form a solid foundation that will support their advice and recommendations given to dog owners, professional dog trainers must make themselves aware of the correlated relationship of wolf and dog behavior and apply it when needed to address problems. They must do this because every behavioral issue they will face with dogs can be explained and remedied if they start with the wolf and bring it forward. Here are a few more examples of this:

Jumping on us. There is nothing that irritates dog owners more than when their dog jumps on them or their friends. If I were given a dollar for every time I have had to address jumping, I would be able to hop in my shiny, red Ferrari after writing this chapter! In fact, I have never known of a dog owner whose dog did not jump on him or her. Why? Jumping is a behavior that is directly attached to survival by wolves, and survival behaviors usually don't become extinct until the species does.

Very young wolf cubs jump up and lick adult wolves on their muzzles. This is a ritual that leads to the adult wolf regurgitating solid food to feed the cubs whose teeth are too underdeveloped to eat directly from a fresh kill. As the young cubs continue to develop, a face-to-face greeting is used to identify other pack members through sight recognition and scent glands located behind the ears on the cheek next to the corner of the mouth. If you happen to be a submissive wolf, it is imperative you recognize a dominant wolf and display the appropriate pacifying behaviors; otherwise, be prepared for one-on-one instruction in wolf etiquette. Such lessons usually come hard and fast!

A very similar instinct drives our dogs to want to be face level with us, too (hence the jumping). The problem is that we are vertical, not horizontal, wolves. Depending upon the size of the dog and the size of the human, achieving a head level status can require serious jumping abilities! If we were to crawl around our dogs on all fours, jumping would decrease greatly because our dogs would easily be able to reach our faces. Too often, when confronted with this issue, professional dog trainers who are not versed in wolf behavior will instruct their clients to turn their backs on their jumping dogs and ignore them. This may work for a small child, but to your domestic wolf, it only causes frustration and confusion because a behavior considered vital to them is made more difficult. Worse yet, turning away from your dog who is confronting you is mimicking a pacifying behavior common to submissive wolves when they are yielding to more dominant wolves. That's it! Turn your back and show them who's the boss! Your dog will appreciate this.

Digging. Personally, I would be fine with my dog digging up the occasional mole that is rampaging my yard, but unfortunately, it never ends there. If left unchecked, most of our yards would resemble a WWI battlefield in no time.

Digging is one of the many destructive behaviors professional dog trainers like to attribute to boredom, and their answer to the problem is to give the dog a greater amount and variety of toys to entertain the dog and distract it from the consistent prodding of the self-preservation instinct that is the real reason why dogs dig; they're hunting. Why are they hunting in your freshly manicured back yard? Well, they are driven by the need to locate sources of energy. Life, at its most primal form, is about obtaining energy. Should you or your dog fail at this acquisition, neither of you will survive for more than a few weeks. Even though you feed your dog one to three meals per day, your dog is not sure this will continue. They understand that you, the kitchen, and the dog bowl are sources of energy, but they have no clue you will continue to be the lifelong benefactor you promised. Hunting for the mole or squirrel or chipmunk in your back yard is reinforcing the life-sustaining skills that could possibly be called upon should your promise fail to hold up. This is why providing your dog with toys to play with may curb some of your dog's digging, but it won't stop it all together.

Coming when called. Teaching your dog to reliably come to you *when you want it to* is one of the most important but challenging tasks you will ever face as a dog owner. The reason lies with the fact that this is not a natural behavior among wolves. There are many reasons why a wolf may howl, bark, or yip. Some of these include the purpose of attracting a mate, to send up a location beacon, or to gather others for a hunt. However, there is no purpose that would drive an *individual* wolf to *demand* that another *individual* wolf stop whatever it is doing at that moment and come to it. If the demanding wolf has a pressing issue with the other wolf, it will go to it. When an individual wolf responds to the vocal cry of another wolf and joins that wolf, it does so out of free will and because it serves some purpose for it, not because it's being made to do so by the other wolf. Sound familiar?

All of our dogs, like wolves, come to us occasionally if it suits *their* need. In order to teach your dog to come when it suits *your* need, you will have to introduce a concept that is lost to your dog because there is no natural instinct to draw upon. This behavior is a human desire carved out of a human world, and it will have to be *forced* upon your dog to achieve the reliability that could possibly save its life and your bank account someday.

Some professional trainers not familiar with wolf behavior will approach the training of "come when called" from the angle of *want* vs. *need*. They will suggest that you offer up a dandy treat or an irresistible toy to persuade your dog to come to you. They are hoping your dog will *want* to come to you, and occasionally, they'll be right. But, as long as you keep providing your dog with food and shelter and the world keeps providing things far more stimulating than a toy, there will never be a *need* for them to come when called. If you want to teach your dog to come to you *every time* you call it under any condition that your lifestyle would provide, you will have to incorporate a *need*, and the *need* will have to come in the form of avoiding something unpleasant if it doesn't come.

In his book, *How the Dog Became a Dog: From Wolves to Our Best Friend*, Mark Derr explains the following:

> *"For all the refinement that breeders have brought to the dog's appearance, the purebred dog still has paws, claws, and a jaw. They may not be as powerful or*

efficient as those of the wolf, but they are there,
and they define the way the dog approaches its world." 8

Our approach to controlling and managing our client's dogs must be the same as the dog's approach to our world. If a professional trainer or behaviorist labels him or herself as an expert, then he or she had better understand this and possess the knowledge, experience, and skills necessary to give expert advice. Anything short of that is negligent and possibly even criminal as the consequences of this fundamental aspect can be more far-reaching than just the dog's unruly behavior.

We need to not make training horribly complicated and beyond the understanding of the average dog owner. There is no need for big words and sophisticated strategies or resumes that go on for miles. My personal experience has shown that my clients were far more impressed when I gave them something they could achieve than when they were shown my curriculum vitae. We just need to keep in mind that every dog problem has a beginning, and that beginning lies first with nature. Every problem can be explained and solved by understanding the three fundamental parts of the equation: the wolf part, the dog part, and the human part. It is every bit as simple as nature intended. You just have to know all of the parts.

———

One day, while we were performing routine maintenance on the gear we often took on our excursions into the wild, my mentor completely disassembled the Model 94, lever action, Winchester rifle I always carried for protection from dangerous predators such as bears and instructed me to put it back together in thirty minutes. The time limit came and went and left me hopelessly lost among the many parts of my rifle. There was no way I was going to be able to put my rifle back together again and not have it blow up in my face when I attempted to shoot it. Seeing this, my mentor took a seat next to me, and as he began to reassemble the eighty plus parts of my rifle, he said, *"You know how to load, aim, and fire this weapon, kid, but you can't tell me where each component belongs, let alone the purpose of each component."* Ashamed, I had to agree with him. I had never taken my rifle completely apart other than the few pieces required to clean and maintain the weapon. My mentor continued, *"If this rifle fails you in the wild, knowing the purpose of each and every part required for firing and where they belong will make the difference between a successful repair or your rifle being reduced to a club."* After pausing a few moments to allow this lesson to sink in, he quietly added, *"To know how to solve any problem in this world, kid, whether it be with your rifle, your family, or with nature, you have to break the problem down to each and every part, learn the purpose of each part, repair the individual parts that are broken, and then put the parts back together again where they belong."* Ten minutes later when he handed me my ready-to-fire rifle, he also handed me a lesson that has served me well in my life. Five years later, my mentor died in combat in Vietnam, and I guarantee you, his rifle had all of its parts in all of the right places, and it was firing.

Know the parts.

The Circles of Life

You have noticed that everything
an Indian does is in a circle, and that is because
the Power of the World always works in circles,
and everything tries to be round...
The Sky is round,
the eyes of the wolf are round,
and I have heard that the earth
is round like a ball,
and so are all the stars.
The wind, in its greatest power, whirls.
Birds make their nest in circles,
for theirs is the same religion as ours...

Even the seasons form a great circle
in their changing and always come back again
to where they were.
The life of a man is a circle from
childhood to childhood, and so it is
in everything where power moves.
~ Black Elk

While sitting in my psychology class in school, I watch as my professor draws several circles on a chalkboard. He inserts symbols in each of the individual circles denoting a man, a woman, and a child. He explains how the circles represent each of us individually and the time and energy it takes to keep ourselves as ourselves. Next, he overlaps the man circle with the woman circle and teaches us about compromising and how much time and energy is needed for the compromise to remain successful. He goes on to state that high levels of stress can possibly be incurred during the process and that stress management would be needed. It all sounds like a lot to me, and I can't help but wonder how much more time and energy expenditure, along with the additional stress, would be needed if you overlapped the man and woman circle with a child circle and a dog circle?

Successful dog ownership, like the one that lowers your blood pressure and doesn't raise it, requires an incredible amount of time and energy, and such time and energy are commodities in short supply in America. Just when you think you've managed to repel all of the other circles overlapping yours, life has a way of sneaking a few in. Your boss needs you to work extra hours to meet a project deadline, and your kid's soccer coach is calling for more practices. The church you attend wants you to help out with the next fundraiser, and your home project list has grown to both sides of the paper. Such is life—it just keeps coming at you, one circle after another.

To make matters worse, the time and energy required for the basic care and training of your dog does not lessen because of your increased personal commitments. Under such conditions, even minimal husbandry duties such as feeding your dog, taking it outside to go potty, and cleaning up after it can create a whole new outlook on the dog circle overlapping yours. Add a few more dog circles to the equation and that outlook suddenly becomes quite clouded. Now imagine if any of the dogs in those circles barked incessantly, made walking it worse than a trip to the dentist, stole the dinner you worked two hours to prepare, chewed a hole in your new sofa, or kept vomiting all over your carpet because you failed to keep it out of the cat's litter box? When these situations are added to all of the other circles life throws at you, it's no wonder all dog owners eventually have one of those moments when they ask themselves, is it really worth it? I know I have!

When I catch myself charting the pros and cons of dog circles invading my life circle, I can't help but be alarmed over the many blogs and essays commonly found on training and veterinary websites. These sources state that even though we live very busy lives, we should take our time and make sure that all care and training be void of any stress on our dogs. Our relationship with our dogs should have but one, anointed goal: the achievement of their unending happiness. Seriously? When did life cease being stressful for dogs? When did a little unhappiness kill them? Trust me, remove any of our dogs from their plush, climate-controlled homes and supplant them in the Alaskan wild in the winter time, and nature and her accompanying stressors will be the landlord of their canine circles.

The question that also begs an answer is what about my stress and my happiness? Since when did the stress and happiness of my dog become more important than mine or my family's? After all, who endures stress and sometimes unhappiness in the pursuit of providing food and shelter so our dogs are not so stressed? Me and you! Don't we count for something in this relationship? Know this: no dog takes up residence in our personal circles for any length of time without the need to address a few of their problem behaviors. So, you can either apply a healthy and efficient dose of stress to your dog to reliably deactivate any of its undesired behaviors or you can live with the stress of not doing so. The choice is yours.

What amazes me is the number of dog owners who choose the latter. Influenced by misinformed counselors masquerading as experts who allege that stress is harmful for dogs, some dog owners subject themselves and their families to a life of misery because they simply cannot bear to pressure their dogs into compliance within established boundaries. Forsaking the leadership that nature requires of social predators, they coddle, plead, or bargain with their dogs while those very same dogs effectively adjust their behavior to the lack of authority and dictate life within all of the circles of the household. These owners hide their lack of will behind the walls of denial and excuses they have built to shield themselves from their dog's woeful behavior. If only they would say "enough!" Their newfound leadership would act like a sledgehammer to demolish those walls of denial and excuses, and a vibrant and productive pack relationship would emerge.

I always tell dog owners, "We *want* obedience, but nature *demands* it; she will use any level of stress necessary to achieve it." Wolves, being apex predators in the land of limited resources, were built for stress absorption. Staying alive requires a daily, monumental effort just for the ingestion of life-sustaining energy, and wolves have been the successful bearer of this burden for millions of years. Because our dogs share a biological relationship with the wolf, they inherited the ability to withstand stress, both mentally and physically at levels that easily surpass the assumption of most dog owners. In fact, in the human-to-domestic dog relationship, it's usually the human who stresses about the day-to-day requirements of husbandry and training, not the dog.

For example, locking your dog in a crate or isolating it from you for a few hours a day so you can attend to the needs of your personal and professional circles will not harm it. Most owners, because of the prevailing anthropomorphic attitude associated with dogs, believe their pet will think of such isolation as punishment and be too afraid to incorporate this needed practice for fear their dog will not like them afterwards. These owners should take comfort in knowing wolves do not seek out stimulation or the company of other wolves every hour of their day. Because nature punishes excessive energy expenditure on the part of predators, most predators sleep to conserve calories when not performing meaningful and productive tasks. Dogs that are left by themselves will not think of their circumstance as punishment; instead, they will nap for the greater part of their separation and be ready to go when you return, just like wolves.

The separation of dog owners from their pets for long periods of time, such as boarding, is a stressful event that most owners and their dogs inevitably go through at some point or another. However, it is particularly hard on the owner who has become emotionally dependent upon the dog circle that shares space with his or her personal circle. This type of dependency is real, and its debilitating effect has been witnessed quite often at our training and boarding facility where we provide a board and train option along with other programs.

The board and train option is very popular because most individual's circles in America more closely resemble a kaleidoscope than the letter "O," and this leaves them with no time to train their dogs. As a result, my wife and I devised a program in which we train the dog and then train the owner. The curriculum requires the owner's dog to spend a few weeks with us while it undergoes intensive training to learn the fundamentals of desired behaviors. The majority of the young dogs enrolled in the program initially experience stress that is associated with new surroundings and separation from their pack (family), but they acclimate quickly and are ready to focus on training regime within one to two days. However, this is not the case with the emotionally dependent owner. While many leave our lobby in tears after dropping off their pet, others inundate us with requests for updates and pictures of their dog at all hours of the day and night during their dog's entire stay! We've even had some of these owners call up to seven times in an eight-hour period to check on their dog.

Recently, a client enrolled her five-month-old German Shepherd puppy in one of our popular board and train programs. Within a few hours of her departure, she had already utilized three different forms of communication to check on her pup. She called, e-mailed, and messaged us through Facebook, and even though she received reassurance from our staff that all was well, she didn't believe it and contacted us six more times that day. After three days and over twenty attempts to contact us to inquire about her dog's welfare, we decided to post a cute picture of her pup on Facebook to alleviate any concerns she was still having about her pup's condition. The next day, the client arrived at our facility, unannounced, and demanded to take her dog home. The reason for her action was because the picture that was posted on Facebook showed her young German Shepherd with one ear standing erect and the other ear down. When we tried to explain this was very common among big boned German Shepherd puppies and had nothing to do with his emotional state, the client informed us that we obviously did not know anything about dogs, let alone her puppy. She declared his ear was down "because he missed his mommy."

This type of panic, which results from owners believing their dog misses them as much as they miss their dog, is caused by both an irrational and maladaptive perception of reality and an underlying emotional disorder. The overall effect on the well-being of dogs in cases such as this one is extremely harmful and much too commonplace among many of today's dog owners.

I was arguing my viewpoint on such behavior with a very prominent dog breeder when she stated, "I would rather the owner of one of my pups care too much than too little." I could not disagree more and went on to explain to her that "caring too much" created a condition that was every bit as harmful as not caring enough. When we become the proverbial "helicopter dog owner," we stifle our dog's true nature and try to make them conform to standards that are in line with our selfish human needs and not their natural wolf-like needs.

Remember the wisdom of the Alaskan Indian when he said, "Treat him like a wolf, and he will run faster and with more spirit." Take your dog into the wild or to a dog park and observe how he instantly becomes excited and overjoyed. That's because those conditions allow the wolf in your dog to surface, uninhibited as he runs faster and with more spirit. Protecting a dog and nurturing it like a human baby is a flagrant discredit to its natural ancestry and only serves to benefit the pitiable human that the dog suffers under.

Such excessive emotions leave you feeling both sorry and deeply concerned for the owner. All too often, the love of our dogs allows their circles to completely overshadow our circles, leading to the poor decision-making and indecisive leadership that places thousands of other dogs and people in harm's way every year.

Such was the case when a lady asked me to help her introduce a four-year-old male Pit Bull she had adopted to her three other dogs. When I arrived at her home, I was shocked by what I saw. Standing before me was a powerful, muscle-bound Pit Bull with several pale scars adorning its body that gave testimony to the many battles it had survived in the dog fighting arena. While looking past the Pit Bull at this lady's other dogs, which included two small, female Labs and an older male Spaniel mix behind a baby gate, I asked, "Why did you adopt this dog?" She replied, with much pride, that the rescue organization from which she had obtained the dog had been unsuccessful in locating a home for it. Fearing the dog may be euthanized, she convinced the rescue group that she was more than able to provide a safe and loving home for the dog. She then went on to boast about how her supreme humanitarian efforts had saved the lives of her other three dogs and this Pit Bull was going to be an addition to her well-earned adoption portfolio.

I was too astonished to speak for several minutes. I thought to myself, have we lost our minds as dog owners? Will we soon lose our minds as parents and bring home mountain lions for our children to play with? The dog circle that was this Pit Bull was a black and foreboding sphere that was not welcome in this home. Surfacing from my dark thoughts, I looked this lady square in the eyes and told her I would not help her introduce her Pit Bull to her other dogs. "Why not?" she asked. With all the sincerity I could muster, I said, "Because you have invited death into your home. It did not come on a pale horse; it came in the form of a Pit Bull. This dog is incompatible with your other dogs, and if you keep him, a tragedy will occur." I then offered to take the Pit Bull from her and personally return it to the rescue organization from which it had come. Taking my recommendation as a personal affront to her errorless decision-making, the lady became very angry and asked me to leave. On my way to my car, she reminded me I wasn't the only trainer in town. Sadly, she was right, and with the approval of another trainer, she kept the Pit Bull who then, in less than a week, killed her Spaniel mix and sent the lady to an intensive care unit with over 200 stitches in her body.

There is no altruism in the wild so its moral practices were not passed from the wolf to the dog. This Pit Bull gave no thought to the graciousness this lady extended in trying to save its life. Like a wolf, it simply eliminated an alien competitor in the Spaniel mix and then attempted to eliminate a threat when the lady tried to break up its attack on the Spaniel with a broom. This can be a very difficult concept to accept as a dog owner, but to accept otherwise can lead to disaster. If we continue to approach dog ownership in the unrealistic sense that the dog's stress-free life of happiness should take precedence over proper placement in households and proper control of its behavior, we are doomed. Nature does not allow for a stress-free existence.

———————

Sweat was pouring down my face and dripping on the map I was holding in one hand and the note, I was staring at in disbelief, in the other. I had just hiked my butt over twelve kilometers through some of the toughest terrain Alaska has to offer to reach a waypoint that had been set by my mentor earlier that morning. The waypoint I was standing on was supposed to have been the end of the exercise, but now I was holding a note left by my mentor on a fallen log that was telling me otherwise. I could just imagine him laughing at what he knew would be my reaction when I read the note.

"Congratulations on reaching this first waypoint. The coordinates below are those of a new waypoint where you will find me. I'll have a warm fire and breakfast waiting for you when you arrive, but if you don't want to miss breakfast and find just another set of coordinates waiting for you, I'd suggest you quit fretting about your new-found circumstances and get to humpin it. Listen, kid, you're gonna get plenty tired, so remember to steady your compass, your pace, your water intake, and, most of all, your attitude. See you in the A.M."

Steady my attitude? I was so mad at that moment my hands were shaking. I rationalized I should steady them first, so I would be able to accurately determine the new waypoint on my map. Spreading the map on the ground, I made my standard adjustments with my compass to allow for magnetic declination, and then I carefully plotted a course to the way-point my mentor had instructed in the coordinates he'd left. Up to that point in my life, I had never cussed, but I found a few of the words I'd heard my mentor say, when he was really mad, forming on my lips when I realized his new coordinates were twenty kilometers away! Not just twenty kilometers but twenty damn, hard kilometers! Looking up at the late September sun that was already low in its zenith, I realized it was going to be a long, cold, and dark journey that would require a fast overnight pace to make it to my mentor's camp in time for breakfast. Just like my mentor wrote in his note, *"I'd suggest you quit fretting and get to humpin it."* I figured I should do just that and at least get moving. After all, I had an entire lonely night to fret.

"What's for breakfast?" I asked my mentor who was sitting, with his back to me, on a piece of deadwood tending to his cooking over a small fire.

"Your favorite: fried spam; scrambled, powdered eggs; and biscuits fresh off the griddle." He'd made no effort to turn around and congratulate me for managing to make it on time as he answered. Instead, he'd just gone about casually preparing breakfast as though we had been together the entire time. I was cold, way beyond tired, and way beyond irritated.

Getting to the spot where he was casually making breakfast had required precise navigation in the dark, without food, across four marshlands full of water and mud, through thickets a rhino would have balked at, up and down too many hills to count, all while carrying a rucksack full of rocks to make it weigh half my body weight. I had just accomplished what most of the adult soldiers he trained couldn't have accomplished. If I ever deserved a *"well done"* or a slap on the back from my mentor, it was right then.

"What's it gonna be, kid? You gonna just stand over there or are you gonna set down your gear and come eat? You've gotta be starving by now." My mentor had turned and was staring at me. Without waiting for me to answer, he scooped up some scrambled eggs and began chewing on them.

"I'm not hungry," I answered. Actually, I was starving, but I was too mad for a "buddy breakfast" at that moment. I didn't want to give him the pleasure of seeing any weakness in me.

"What you need right now, kid, is food. What you don't need right now is a bunch of words telling you what a great job you did. Like, how you hung in there and persevered when most grown men would have quit. No sir, what you need is energy to replace the energy you spent getting here if you want to have enough energy to get outta here. Now, get over here and eat because I have no intention of carrying you back home." No matter how mad I was, I knew when to say uncle, and sensing the "real" message that came with my mentor's last order, I said uncle and took up a seat on the ground next to the fire opposite of him. As he handed me a plate with a heaping pile of scrambled eggs and fried spam, he quietly asked, *"When a wolf humps it the same distance you traveled to get here, through the same marshes and thickets looking for food, does he fret over it?* Pausing to swallow my mouth full of eggs, I answered, "no sir." He then continued, *"When that same wolf, after going through what you went through yesterday and last night, manages to run down a mule deer and kill it, does anyone congratulate him?"* "No sir," I managed as I sensed where his questioning was going. *"That's right, kid. He doesn't pout because no other wolves are there to witness his great hunting*

skills and howl all night to proclaim his glory. Instead, he eats so he will have the energy to do it again and again for the rest of his life." He paused long enough for me to give what he had just said some thought and for me to finish my breakfast. As he reached for my empty plate and began wiping it with a rag, I looked him in the eyes and said, "I'm sorry about my attitude, sir. I understand nature has no room for egos." He simply replied, *"No, she doesn't, kid. Nature keeps it simple that way. Man makes things way too complicated with his ego."*

Later that morning, after allowing me a short nap, my mentor and I began the long trek back home. A few kilometers into our journey, we stopped while he took an updated bearing with his compass. "What was the purpose of adding another twenty kilometers to the exercise yesterday, and why the secrecy?" The question had been gnawing at me since after breakfast, but I had fallen asleep before I could ask it. As I had stood behind him watching him sight through his compass, I had been reminded, and I was curious to find out.

"Stress. It's as simple as that. Life doesn't always warn you ahead of time about those things that will cause you stress, and when you came across my note, it definitely caused you to become stressed. It's important to practice absorbing stress and overcoming it so that when you get hit with it, overcoming it is what you do naturally. Nature stresses wolves every day, and every day, they absorb it naturally. What other choice do they have? Nothing gets to go through life without stress, kid—you, me, and wolves included. No matter what stressors you encounter in life, keep it simple like wolves—absorb, move, hunt, eat. Say it, kid: absorb, move, hunt, eat." As he folded his compass, my mentor turned back to face me. His face was weathered and tanned from the summer sun, and I could

barely make out his eyes under the brim of his hat. The line that creased his face was a smile, and all of the anger I had felt towards him left me with a stressor that I would never come to absorb naturally: guilt.

"Absorb, move, hunt, eat, sir," I answered with pride.

"Congratulations, kid. You did a hell of a job with this challenge. You encountered stress, absorbed it, and overcame it." I couldn't help but smile, but before my ego could get too big, nature intervened.

"Here's my compass, kid. Our next waypoint is the coordinates listed on this note. Lead the way." I took his note and plotted our course to the new waypoint on my map. Of course, it was twenty kilometers. Absorb, move, hunt, eat. Keep it simple.

My mentor was correct in his prediction: "No one will get out of this world without stress." Therefore, during my life, I have come to understand the importance of stress management when too many other circles begin to overlap my own. For the most part, the management of personal circles can be accomplished relatively easily with a little extra energy, ingenuity, and a "can do" attitude. Such management can oftentimes be accomplished by keeping it simple like the wolf, but sometimes it may include repelling unnecessary circles, prioritizing the needs of others, or in the worst case, expanding your personal circle so it can hold more circles. However, managing dog circles is much more difficult because options that work well for your personal circle don't work well with your dog's. For instance, repelling your dog circle would require euthanasia or rehoming your dog, and this tends to add even more stress to your personal circle. Dog circles, by nature, are needy circles because of their intrinsic husbandry and training requirements; prioritizing around them becomes nearly impossible. The only option that seems to work is the option that nature says we should never select: expanding our personal circle to allow our ever-expanding dog circle to fit in.

Wolves have been labeled as the *champions of compromise* by many ethologists. However, this title was earned through a backdoor approach in that wolves own very selfish personal circles. They only allow the overlapping of other wolves' circles because it benefits their own personal circle. In the case of hunting a large herbivore, you will need many wolves to bring it down; throw one rabbit into the midst of a hungry wolf pack and see how much compromising the most dominant wolf does as he swallows the rabbit! In other words, the wolf (and our dog) will only compromise as long as it suits its own personal circle. It will never expand its circle to allow for our expanding needs. This simply doesn't fit in with the law of self-preservation that is the number one priority in predatory circles.

We are in desperate need of a new attitude in our approach to dog ownership. We should not permit our dogs to cause us physical or emotional pain, to stress our human relationships to a breaking point, or to endanger our way of life because we believe the welfare of their circle should be considered before ours. We are humans, and we live on earth where we were given dominion over the creatures that inhabit it. Our dogs should only be accepted into our personal circles by our invitation. Through the eyes of the alpha wolf, this acceptance is conveyed daily to his pack. Because of this, his pack doesn't merely adhere to his boundaries, it thrives!

Copy the last paragraph and tape it to your refrigerator. Keep the following in mind: if you add a little stress and perhaps a little unhappiness to your dog's life, it will adapt to this input as readily and as graciously as the wolf. I guarantee it will lead to a little less stress and a whole lot more happiness in your dog.

Such are the circles of life.

The Hammer

Dark spruce forest frowned on either side
the frozen waterway. The trees had been stripped by a
recent wind of their white covering of frost,
and they seemed to lean toward each other,
black and ominous, in the fading light.
A vast silence reigned over the land.
The land itself was a desolation, lifeless,
without movement, so lone and cold that
the spirit of it was not even that of sadness.
There was a hint in it of laughter,
but of a laughter more terrible
than any sadness—a laughter
that was mirthless as the smile of the Sphinx,

a laughter cold as the frost and partaking
of the grimness of infallibility. It was the masterful
and incommunicable wisdom of eternity
laughing at the futility of life and the effort of life.
It was the Wild, the savage, frozen-hearted Northland Wild.
~ Jack London, White Fang

The wife tearfully pets their young, male dog while her husband fidgets and nods his head slowly. "So that's it, huh?" he asks. "That's it, zero percent," I answer, affirming his understanding of the chances I figure these parents have of their dog not severely biting one or both of their children again in the very near future. My reply is without emotion and straight to the point. It has to be, or the all too important message will be lost in translation. I need to extinguish any hope these parents have of owning the dog safely around their five-year-old twins. In the past, when I utilized a more tactful approach, owners of aggressive dogs somehow managed to take my warnings and turn them into sympathetic loopholes that were then used to justify their disregard of my recommendations. As a result, a lot of people, both young and old, earned a trip to the nearest emergency room.

I arrived at this conclusion after a lengthy interview of the parents and the events leading up to the attack. I also conducted a thorough evaluation of their dog where diagnostic tests revealed that the dog's perception of children was that of a threat even when children offered him treats. The dog had been adopted two years earlier as a puppy from a rescue, and a recent bite to one of the twins had led the parents to seek my advice. During the interview, I explained that nearly fifty percent of children are bitten by a dog before they reach the age of thirteen. I also informed them that their children were in the age group (five to nine years old) that is most often bitten as recorded by the United States Centers for Disease Control and Prevention. 9 Their children would also still be in this age group long after their dog matured in both physical and emotional stature where aggression would evolve into a much more perilous condition. Lastly, I explained that due to the inherent unpredictability of their children's behavior with their dog, who was extremely fearful and viewed the children as a threat, it was certain one of the children would be bitten again. To keep the children safe, the dog would have to go. There was no other way out.

"I don't get it. This dog grew up with our kids, and everything was perfectly fine until the last month when he turned two. I can't believe he would suddenly think one of our five-year-old sons was threatening him and feel the need to bite him," the wife pleaded. Her response is very typical to the one I receive when I counsel parents about dog aggression and their children. Because they imagine their dog as part of their family, they can't come to grips with the fact that their dog, who grew up with their children, would ever cause them harm. Along the same lines, it is also difficult for them to comprehend the speed with which most dogs achieve full emotional and physical maturity when compared with their children. In the same time it takes a child to go from infant to toddler, a dog goes from puppy to full blown adult. As an adult, life and everything in it, including young children, are taken seriously by our dogs. As with the wolf, it is a time in which every choice results in either a positive move towards its future survival or a many layered consequence. Kids who were once viewed as playmates are now viewed as opponents or threats. Parents, once followed, are now challenged. If pressed, the adult domestic dog will call to action a means to solve its problem: aggression. This trait is the lifeblood of the wolf and often leaves parents shocked and children scarred for life.

Aggression is the most dominant tool in the wolf's bag of survival equipment. Nature did not give them diplomacy, contracts, mediators, or negotiations. She gave them a hammer. It is a mechanism, thousands of years in the making, tempered for social predators to eliminate or control competitors, obtain life-sustaining energy, acquire a mate, and secure a safe dwelling place to raise offspring and withstand the assault of other predators. It is the guardian of the ingestion, reproduction, and preservation necessary for the continuance of its species. It is as necessary and commonplace to the wolf's survival as the very air which it breathes.

Dogs carry a hammer as well. It may not be as big and ominous as the wolf's, but it is still the dominant tool in their bag. A common example of dogs using their hammer is often seen at dog parks when a naive owner throws a tennis ball into the midst of several dogs at play. When more than one dog wants the tennis ball, they do not draw straws; play rock, paper, scissors; or create a time-sharing plan to see who gets the ball. The dog that is most dominant among the interested dogs will either seize the tennis ball first or use aggression to take the ball away from any competitor. It will then use aggression to keep the ball. Hammer time!

Domestic dogs are commonly provided a safe territory, in the form of a home, and plenty of food to eat. Therefore, the hammer that is needed by a wolf in the acquisition of such is not always *needed* by our dogs. Because most of these dogs are either spayed or neutered, the hammer is also not *needed* for the perpetuation of their species as they don't often find themselves in competition for fertile mates. The domestic dog, as a species, continues because humans, for the most part, provide for the basic needs of ingestion, safe dwelling places, and reproduction through breeding programs and unaltered dogs. Because we do this, aggression as a whole may not be utilized by our dogs as often or at the same intensity as that of the wolf. However, it is still the "go to" tool for many of the same reasons. Ironically, because of our beneficence, the top two reasons for aggression are both associated with self-preservation —one in the form of controlling competitors and the other in the form of deliverance from possible attacks.

Without delving deep into the specifics of the evolution of predatory social behavior, I will keep it short and say that nature intended for groups of wolves to band together in a concerted effort to survive and thrive in a hostile environment. However, the basic survival needs of any individual must be met before that individual is able to contribute to the survival needs of others; this is called self-preservation. To avert the more powerful wolves of the group from killing the weaker wolves of the group for the purpose of self-preservation, nature instilled a social awareness. She said to the powerful wolves, "It would not be wise to kill the weaker wolves of your group because you will need those wolves to help you obtain enough food to keep yourself alive for the many long months of winter." So, the more powerful and dominant wolves heeded nature's advice and learned to work with the weaker and more submissive wolves. In the process, the more powerful and dominant wolves not only obtained enough food for their individual survival, they also contributed to the survival of their weaker helpers by allowing them to eat what was left over. In cases when there weren't enough leftovers to feed all of the weaker helpers, some went without. Positioning oneself within the group suddenly became very important to ensure you got enough to eat, and from this, a hierarchy was born.

In the wild, the higher one's status in the hierarchy, the more opportunity a wolf has to eat and have a mate. This not only benefits the high-ranking individual but also the species as a whole because a stronger gene pool continues to be passed on to the next generation. The drive to achieve top positioning is not as powerful in domestic dogs because of the lack of urgency associated with spending a lifetime on the brink of starvation like wolves. However, it still exists and is typical of dogs born of dominant genes. These dogs, even when showered with love, will sometimes employ aggression, like the wolf, to achieve an enhancement in hierarchical status among the weaker humans and dogs they view as competitors in the same household. They will then use their elevated position to forcefully take and protect food and other items. Should human or dog fail to give way to them, an attack will certainly result. This is done not because they are starving or because they don't like you or the other dogs but because of the persistent whispering of nature telling them, "When it comes to self-preservation, it pays to be a winner."

Luckily for wolves, dogs, and mankind, nature did not produce only dominant genes. Always striving for a perfect balance among social predators, she produced submissive genes to keep competition stabilized and in check. Otherwise, too many dominant genes would have led to too much competition, which would then have led to too many competitors being eliminated; eventually, there would have been too few wolves, dogs, and humans needed for survival. When the phrase, "All men were created equal," was penned by our fore-fathers, thank goodness they got it wrong. If nature had created only dominant humans, we would have eradicated our species a long time ago in our pursuit of world dominance.

Lower ranking wolves usually comprise those with the submissive genes. Submissive genes tend to make the recipient a bit more insecure and less driven to reign over the pack. Where the dominant wolf's aggression is more offensive, the submissive wolf's aggression is more defensive in its pursuit of self-preservation. Because of this passive trait, submissive wolves mostly resort to aggression only if confronted with an endangering situation or when defensive mechanisms such as pacifying behaviors, immobility, or flight fail to work. The aggression utilized is often just potent enough to secure the capability of flight where none previously existed.

This type of defensive aggression is commonly known as "fear aggression" among our domestic dogs, and it accounts for a major portion of the 4.5 million dog bites that are reported each year in the United States. This is a staggering and unacceptable number, and the cause of such is attributable to both a rapidly weakening gene pool that has created a very fearful dog and poor decision-making on the part of benighted owners who fail to recognize when their dog feels threatened and understand what to do when they are. It is difficult to prevent a dog attack if you never see it coming and you don't know what proper actions to take when you do. Couple this with the fact that fearful dogs are far more likely to interpret a non-family dog or human as a threat and react with aggression. Therefore, you can easily account for the high number of bites that occur each year.

The blame for not recognizing why and when your dog feels threatened can be placed mostly on human misperceptions of encounters; on the other hand, not knowing how to safely manage a fearful dog can be blamed on the volumes of misguided information available to dog owners.

Let us address the issue of human misperception first.

Most owners, in regard to their dog, fail to understand that perception, by nature, is individual. Thinking your dog will always perceive its world, including the humans and the other dogs that dwell in it, the same as you is very unrealistic and very unsafe. To even remotely accomplish this, your dog would have to be human and harbor the same prejudices and convictions as you do. It would also have to assume that all other humans and dogs will conform to the same rules and boundaries as established by your moral consciousness.

Because this will never be the case, you have to remain open-minded to the fact that your dog may perceive a strange dog or human quite differently than you. You must always remain alert, for there is very little leverage when it comes to accessing your dog's perception accurately; should your dog view the other dog or human as a threat, aggression may be utilized to solve its predicament. If aggression is used, it will be dispensed with the same speed and ease that Starbucks uses to dispense coffee. Not being prepared for this will leave you caught unaware and unable to prevent a bite.

A student of mine and his four-month-old Lab puppy learned through their own self-discovery just how painful such a misperception can be. They were attending their first group obedience class, and I had just given a speech to all the participants about the perception of domestic dogs and how similar their views were to wolves. In the speech, I had emphasized how important it was to defer to their dogs in regard to their approach or avoidance of the other dogs or humans in the class. I told them to never drag their dog by its leash to meet another dog. In such a case, the dog being dragged would be trying, but failing, to adhere to the *"don't get near me"* signals being emanated by the opposing dog. To force the meeting could result in an attack by either dog.

My student with the Lab puppy must have failed to hear or understand my instructions because he clearly did not heed them. While I was focused on the other half of the class socializing their dogs, I suddenly heard from behind me a very loud pop followed by the high pitched screaming of the Lab puppy and two women in the class. As I whirled around, I almost ran into the student who had his Lab puppy cradled in his arms. There was blood everywhere. The pup was sporting a very nasty gash over his right eye, and he was missing over half of his right ear. I later learned from the class that when the Lab puppy had pulled back on his leash to avoid meeting a large, male dog, his owner had exclaimed, "Come on, you little wimp. He looks like a nice enough chap!" And then he had proceeded to lift up his pup and carry him over to meet the male dog, face to face. When they got close, the male dog lunged and bit the Lab pup.

Misperception led to this pup being scarred for life. The owner had made two incorrect assumptions based on his "human" perception of the other dog and that of his own. His first incorrect assumption occurred when he saw a large, male dog sitting very still next to his female owner, and he assumed the dog had to be friendly because he was so well behaved. He was not aware that the dog was extremely fearful of him and his pup, and having perceived both as a threat, had elected the defensive mechanism of immobility at their approach. This mechanism is utilized by predators when they discern other predators at a distance but quickly approaching. It is a brief moment in which their IFF (Identification: Friend or Foe) is activated. In the case of a dominant wolf or dog, identification of a foe may result in an attack. With the submissive wolf or dog, identification of a foe will likely result in flight if it is an option. Because the large, male dog was in a group obedience class, the option of flight was eliminated by his owner's very secure grip on the required leash that was connected to him.

The second incorrect assumption occurred when the student believed his pup, who was trying not to go near the large, male dog, was just being a wimp. He failed to realize that his pup, who was ignorant of human perception but well versed in canine perception, had already recognized the warning signals clearly being sent by the opposing dog and was trying desperately to exercise his avoidance option. Thinking he could inject a bit of courage by forcing his dog into a meeting, the pup's owner literally fed his pup to the other dog. The male dog, suddenly confronted by threats in the form of a big man and another dog that had instantly grown much larger than he, employed the only means he had left to solve his predicament. He attacked.

The inaccuracy of dog owner perception has contributed greatly to the rapid advancement of dog attacks in the United States but not as much as the ill-advised information given to dog owners by those masquerading as behavioral experts.

As I explained in Chapter 6, people who think they can train a dog can print business cards, develop a website, and label themselves as behavioral experts. This is a common practice with many different businesses such as painting, home repairs, landscaping, etc. However, the consequences of erroneous information given to dog owners by uneducated or wrongly taught dog trainers can be far more serious than the wrong color painted on your walls or your plants being pruned too short. Bestowing the label of "expert" on oneself and peddling the wrong advice to an owner whose dog has shown aggressive behavior in the past might lead to someone being severely bitten, possibly even to death.

For over thirty years, I have had veterinarians, professional dog trainers, rescue groups, attorneys, and even universities refer thousands of clients to me in order to help them successfully gain control and manage their aggressive dogs. Most of these clients had previously sought a consultation with a behavioral expert regarding their particular case, and the majority had not been given proper advice. In fact, had they been given sound advice early on, most of these cases would not have required my assistance. Deactivation of certain mechanisms early in the onset of aggression would have resulted in the dog making the necessary adjustments to its behavior before continued success with aggression would have done its damage and become the *modus operandi* for dealing with life's surprises.

All too often, some of today's professional dog trainers are just as confused about the proper methods needed to adjust and instill behaviors in dogs required to coexist safely in the human realm as the very client who is paying them for their expertise. Again, this is attributable to our refusal to accept that our dogs are still very much like wolves in their approach to dealing with us and other dogs.

To demonstrate this, I recall a time when a client called to ask advice on how to deal with the threatening behaviors her dog was displaying whenever the client entered the kitchen while her dog was eating. She said her dog would growl menacingly and show its teeth if she got within ten feet of it. Before I could discuss her case, she went on to tell me about the advice she had already received from a dog trainer employed at a local pet store. The trainer had instructed her to rub her hands all over her dog's food bowl and even in the food itself the next time she prepared her dog's meal. By doing this, she would leave her scent on the bowl and the food. Her dog would detect her owner's scent, know her owner had prepared the food, and be eternally grateful. In return, her dog would no longer growl at her. I asked my client how this had worked out for her. Her reply was, "My dog bit me."

Another example of poor advice given by a behavioral expert who misperceived the situation involves the hotly debated topic as to whether dogs should be allowed to sleep in bed with their owners. Most behavioral experts are not in favor of this as they fear this privilege could erode the owner's leadership. At the end of the day, I have no issue with dogs sleeping in your bed until your dog has an issue with "you" sleeping in your bed. If that's the case, you are either dealing with a very dominant dog and leadership erosion or you are dealing with a deeper problem where the dog's perception of your partner is that of a threat. In both scenarios, aggression is often employed by the dog to achieve its objective or solve its problem.

In the particular case I speak of, a newlywed couple's marriage was unnecessarily strained by the unsound recommendations they received from an expert they had paid quite handsomely to provide a solution to their dog-in-the-bed problem.

The wife usually retired earlier than her husband because of her work schedule, and when she went to bed, the three-year-old male spaniel she had owned prior to the marriage did, too. This posed no problem for the first few days of living and sleeping together, but after that, any time the husband tried to climb into bed, the dog attacked him. This did not sit too well with the new husband, so it wasn't long before they consulted the aforementioned behavioral expert for advice. "The dog belonged to her (the wife), and she belonged to him (the dog) before the two of you were married. They were mates before the two of you were mates. The dog is understandably jealous of you, the new husband, and just needs time to adjust to this new arrangement," he explained to the husband. The expert then proceeded to instruct them on how best to deal with this very sensitive issue by saying, "I recommend the husband sleep in the guest bedroom until the dog is comfortable with the husband taking up residence in the master bed again. Do this for at least thirty days before attempting to sleep with your wife. If the dog continues to show aggression, you must immediately retreat to the guest bedroom and repeat the process every thirty days thereafter." The only good thing that came from this advice was the opportunity for the new husband to find out early in the marriage who was more important to his new bride—him or the dog!

Weeks later, I had the opportunity to interview this couple. While doing so, I learned the new husband was former military and a strict disciplinarian. His initial assessment of his bride's dog was that of a spoiled brat. Although he was probably not far off the mark, his attempt to "whip the dog into shape" in two days was too much and too fast for a dog that exhibited submissive characteristics. The husband's two-day boot camp certainly produced a better behaved dog, but it also produced a fearful perception of him. From that moment forward, every time the husband's six-foot, three-inch imposing frame entered the dark bedroom, it posed a threat for the young Spaniel. Had the behavioral expert been able to recognize this and been educated in the mechanisms employed by wolves and dogs when they encounter a viable threat, he could have explained that the attacks were not motivated by jealousy but rather because the option to flee, which is always chosen first before attacking, was not available. The very dark silhouette of a known threat blocking the only escape route will certainly lead to an attack if the warnings by the dog are not heeded. I explained this to the couple and gave them instructions on how to meld the dog into their new pack existence. Two evenings later, I received a thank you e-mail from the husband that was written while he was in bed with his wife and "their" dog.

As in the case of the Spaniel, dogs take much longer than their human companions to acclimate and become accustomed to the presence of strangers and new surroundings. This timorous nature of theirs has aided in our dogs perceiving the most unlikely things as threats. Dogs inherited this feeling of uneasiness from the wolf whose safety lies within its pack and real danger lies outside its pack in the form of alien wolves or humans. A wolf can be killed by an alien wolf in its attempt to defend its territory or while trying to eliminate a competitor. Even with extremely protective laws, wolves are often killed by hunters or someone who intentionally kills it to defend property and livestock. The perilous nature of such encounters has supplemented the wolf's survival instinct by creating an aloof, antisocial predator out of a very social one.

Curiosity may have killed the cat, but it certainly didn't kill the wolf.

Because survival instincts outlast all others, our dogs, like the wolf, will never be as tolerable with outsiders as they are with our own family pack. When they come in contact with foreign dogs and people, their IFF will automatically kick into gear and the mechanisms of flight and attack will be put on high alert because the possibility of Foe, for obvious reasons, needs to be addressed before the title of Friend can be attached. During any part of the identification process should our dogs perceive the other dog or person as a Foe, they will either try to put distance between themselves and the Foe or they will attack it.

A simple way to observe this is to watch what your dog does the next time a Fedex or UPS delivery person walks up to your door with a package. If your dog has not previously identified the individual as a Friend, Foe will be assumed and your dog will commence with either the mechanism of flight and back away from the door or throw itself at the door with every atom in its body while emitting the most ferocious growl and bark it can muster. Inevitably, the delivery person will go about his business regardless of the actions of your dog and leave. However, your dog, not realizing the invading person has more deliveries to make, will think he motivated the Foe to leave and you can certainly bet if he ever encounters that Fedex or UPS delivery person again, he'll give him more of the same medicine!

Both the wolf and the dog will always repeat the use of aggression in any situation in which success was previously realized from its application. This is why you can be assured the delivery person will receive the same welcome during his next visit to your home. This comes naturally to any predator as nature rewards successes and punishes failures. Case in point, if a wolf tries to capture a vole that is currently occupying a subnivean space (below the snow) using technique A, and fails after several attempts, hunger will drive that same wolf to switch to technique B. If the use of technique B is successful, then technique B will continue to be utilized until the vole population becomes savvy to the wolf's use of technique B and switch their evasiveness to technique C. Such is the ebb and flow of the life of predator and prey.

Another example of how success affects behavior involves domestic dogs when taken for a walk. You and your dog are enjoying a bit of exercise on your daily excursion around the neighborhood when you are confronted with another dog and its owner approaching from a distance. As the gap closes, your dog, perceiving the approaching pair as a possible threat, starts to growl and pull at the end of the leash. It does this because the ever valuable flight option has been eliminated with the use of the leash, leaving your dog with only the option of attack to solve its predicament. You do not realize this and pull back on the leash as hard as you can, all the while reprimanding your dog for its embarrassing behavior. The approaching dog, with its owner glaring at you with an expression of obvious contempt, speeds past you while your dog becomes Hell on four legs and lunges at the other dog with all its might. Within what seems more like hours but is only a few minutes, the pair fades into the distance and your dog finally settles down with you realizing that every time this occurs, your dog seems to be becoming more and more aggressive.

Regrettably, your realization is accurate. Your dog is becoming more aggressive with each and every occurrence such as this because it continues to achieve success in the application of its aggression. Your dog has no clue that the other dog and its owner were not really a threat and that they were traveling on a course that would have taken them past regardless of its behavior. Instead, your dog perceived them as threats and its aggressive actions were successful in thwarting their blatant attack and chasing them off! Bingo! Because nature rewards success, you are guaranteed to go through this again and again should your dog ever perceive the approach of another dog and its owner as a threat. Success begets success.

Because we are human, our IFF system operates in more of a standby mode rather than on high alert like our dogs. Common, everyday events that could possibly be interpreted as a danger by our dogs are not so for us. A neighbor passing by with his or her dog or a stranger asking permission to pet our dog certainly doesn't pose as a threatening situation. Welcomed guests to our homes are just that, welcomed. The purpose of their visit is not to take our homes; they are there by our invitation. Children, the very creatures of human innocence, represent the least danger of all and actually need protection from us and not us from them. Again, we humans simply view things differently than our dogs. Their lives may run in a parallel existence with ours, but their initial interpretation of the other living things in it can be completely opposite. A dog's teeth may not be as sharp as that of a wolf's, but a dog's willingness to use them is every bit as much. When they are used, self-preservation is the intent regardless of what its owner feels about the recipient or perceives the situation to be.

One of the most traumatic and heartbreaking moments for parents occurs when their dog attacks their child. I have stared into the stunned and listless eyes of thousands of parents whose children were seriously injured by a dog. I have listened with empathy as they recounted the exact moment the time of Camelot ended. I have felt the pain that an uncertain future can bring to an all too perfect present. For them, the word "why" becomes a prayer, and life with a dog will never be the same.

Most of the suffering incurred by these parents is caused by their misinterpretation of the events leading up to the attack and the misperceived fantasy of their dog's role in the family that preceded it. As I have mentioned often in this book, the belief held by dog owners that they possess four-legged humans is a major contributor to their problems and the aggression they experience. When we treat and love our dogs like family, we expect the same back. We would expect our children to get into occasional, harmless quarrels over toys, but we would never expect them to have to be taken to a hospital over one. This is exactly what Rocky the Rottweiler does when little Suzy, a three-year-old child, tries to pull her Barbie doll out of his mouth. From a human standpoint, such behavior on the part of Rocky is difficult to understand. But, from a wolf standpoint, it is very easy.

When a wolf encounters another wolf across the way that is approximately the same size, what he sees staring back at him depends greatly upon his genetic make up. If he possesses dominant genes, he is likely to see an opponent. If he possesses submissive genes, he is likely to see a threat. This is known as *the principle of resemblance,* and it plays an instrumental role in the dog-to-child interaction. By the time most children are two years of age, they are either head level with the family dog or slightly taller. When little three-year-old Suzy approaches Rocky, the family dog possessing dominant genes, Rocky doesn't see a child closing in or a family member for that matter; instead, he sees a pack competitor who wants to take his prize. As she nears, he stares her in the eyes and emits a low, threatening growl. He is using natural mechanisms to avoid a confrontation with Suzy because in the wild, all fights are risky and unintended injuries sometimes happen to even the victor. Suzy, just being three years old, fails to recognize the hard stare and the growl for what they are and reaches for the Barbie.

In the bloody aftermath, grieving parents are confounded when Rocky shows no remorse. They can't believe that their beloved family dog could do this to his "sister" and not seek forgiveness. It confounds them further when I tell them Rocky isn't the least bit remorseful and that their concept of redemption doesn't have any value to an animal whose instincts were passed down by a competitor whose instincts were honed by an overwhelming competition for survival in a land of limited resources. To Rocky, he warned, the opponent ignored, he attacked, the opponent left without the doll, and he won. End of story.

The pain we suffer when our children are attacked by the family dog stays with us. It may lessen over time, but its effect is undeniable every time we hear a dog growl. However, the pain associated with the family dog biting a non-family member can be even more devastating when the actions of your dog lands you in court. This is because when such harm is caused by a dog, even in the case of erroneous perception, it is not just the dog that is condemned for its barbaric behavior, the owner is, too. Parents of injured children are quick to direct blame at the aggressive dog with words such as vicious, crazy, and euthanasia embedded in their claim. They also direct the same blame at its owner with words such as lawsuit, compensatory, punitive, liable, and reckless added to the mix. Parents with children bitten by the family dog can be cited by Child Protection Services and labeled as irresponsible, negligent, and even criminal. Emotions abound and chaos ensues as the sights are set on the obvious target—the dog and its owner. It's an open-and-shut case that needs not be made more complicated by considering the fact that the actions of the recipients may have contributed to the outcome or that nature may have played the greatest role. When it comes to a dog attack, it's easier to keep it simple and hang 'em all at noon.

Harboring such an attitude after an attack does nothing to further the tranquil coexistence humans seek with dogs. It will also not prevent our children from being attacked again, and it will certainly not prevent our dogs from attacking when they feel it is necessary to do so. In fact, those children, whose parents are lured into the false sense of security that accompanies the belief they and their child did nothing wrong, are the ones most likely to be involved in a dog attack again. Because nature is both predictable and repetitive, these children, without proper education, will ignorantly wade right into the open jaws of the next dog.

When it comes to human and dog coexistence, there is nothing that will separate the "co" from existence faster than aggression. It is THE part of our relationship with our dogs that does NOT allow for any misperceptions on our part and certainly any attachments of anthropomorphism. I can think of no other topic in regard to dog behavior that warrants more seriousness and consideration, and yet, as typical of human ignorance and denial, it has been explained away and tucked away from an uneducable dog owner society that wishes to see no evil or hear no evil. Wish it or not, if you are a dog owner, you need to pay attention to the following three points:

1. Dog aggression is here to stay. No matter how hard humans try to breed it out, train it out, or medicate it out, it's going nowhere. Regardless as to whether the aggression is used for acquisition or defense, it will continue to be dispensed with an ease by our dogs that is not easily accepted or understood by us. It is a hammer, given by nature to wolves to guard their survival, and under this guardianship, the wolf has risen from merely surviving to a thriving apex carnivore. Like it or not, they passed this hammer on to our dogs. Nature gave it, and only nature can take it away.

2. Our dog's perception is vastly different than ours, and their reaction to non-family dogs and humans of various sizes, shapes, genders, and personalities may vary from one encounter to the next. A peaceful encounter this time does NOT guarantee a peaceful encounter next time.

3. Dog aggression is NOT governed by our laws or our moral consciousness. A dog will NEVER heed a "play fair" sign if it feels the need to attack, and it will NEVER show remorse for doing so. In fact, if your dog gained any perceived advantage for its use, it is guaranteed your dog will use it again under the same circumstances.

Whether your dog is the attacker or the recipient of an attack, do your best to stand outside the bubble of human emotion and prejudice and examine what really occurred. Study it from your dog's and/or the other dog's viewpoint and learn from the experience so that you can either avoid or lessen an aggressive scenario in the future. Do not fear but be comforted by the fact that the use of aggression by our dogs is repetitive and predictable. Because of this, attacks are preventable, and this knowledge is a gift from nature. Use it well.

"Zero percent doesn't leave much room for negotiation," the husband says.

"Not unless you're willing to gamble on your children's safety," I reply.

While gazing at his wife and their dog, he asks me, "I guess we will have to find our dog a new home and one that doesn't have small children?"

"Yes, that is correct," I answer.

I watch as the husband then puts his arm around his wife's shoulder, and I listen to her cry while he tries his best to console her. It often comes down to this: an attack, an evaluation, and an outcome where the dog is made to leave the family. My word is final in most decision-making, and the responsibility of such weighs heavily on me at the moment. This family has invested two years of their lives in this dog, and rehoming is a difficult concept to embrace when you would never rehome one of your children, no matter how terrible he or she became. I can only hope they listened to what I told them about wolves and dogs and why nature equipped them with aggression and why their dog has used and will use the hammer again. If they did, then hopefully they will understand the ultimatum I have presented to them and make the correct and responsible decision to rehome their dog.

"So, if we rehome this dog and apply what we have learned from you today, what are our chances that we will be able to get a new dog and establish a safe and compatible relationship with it and our two children?" I am relieved to hear this question being asked, but I'm caught off guard when I realize it comes from the wife. I study her for a moment, looking for a sign that convinces me she is on board with my recommendation and not just seeking some sort of leverage to change my mind. I notice she is no longer crying and that she has shrugged off her husband's embrace. She has calmed down, and her nervous petting of her dog has subsided. For the first time since meeting her, I now see a mother—first, a wife—second, and a dog owner—last.

"One hundred percent," I answer.

Will

It is nearly impossible for modern man
to imagine what it is like to live by hunting.
The life of a hunter is one of hard, seemingly
continuous overland travel...
A life of frequent concerns
that the next interception may not work,
that the trap or the drive will fail,
or that the herds will not appear this season.
Above all, the life of a hunter carries with it the
threat of deprivation and death by starvation.
~ John M. Campbell, *The Hungry Summer*

The female cheetah sits, unmoving, as she gazes out over the shimmering Serengeti valley. The only detectable movement is the slow rise and fall of her chest as she breathes. I glass the valley with my binoculars, hoping to catch a glimpse of what has her interest, but the heat waves obscure my vision and give no hint. After what seems like hours, she turns her head slowly and faces her two six-month-old cubs, who are sitting motionless at her side. Even though I am a hundred yards away, I can feel an ominous power emanating from the look she is giving them. Whatever message is being passed, it is non-negotiable. She continues staring at her cubs for several seconds while her cubs stare back at her. There is no trace of a challenge or disrespect in their gaze, only acknowledgment.

Then, suddenly, with a purpose driven hotter than the sand beneath her paws, the female cheetah turns and vanishes into the long grass. The cubs make no attempt to follow her. With eyes fixed on the horizon, they remain statue still, with no discernible sound coming from their direction—no whining, no panting, no nothing. An eerie calm has settled over the African plain that holds their attention. As if reacting to a foreboding urgency, the Serengeti has ceased to breathe.

The business of killing is at hand.

_____

As humans, we *want* obedience. Whether it is from our children, our employees, or our dogs, we want it. Nature, however, *requires* it. And I have found there is no place like the Serengeti plains of Africa to observe how serious nature is about it.

In the story above, the female cheetah returns to her cubs dragging a gazelle that she has killed. Even though the hunt has lasted over an hour and has covered a large expanse of territory, it is easy for her to locate them because they are exactly where and as she has left them—sitting still and quiet like statues. The non-negotiable orders, *"Remain here. Do not move or make a sound until I return,"* that were conveyed with just a look before she left have been obeyed. It is not the first time for these cubs, nor will it be the last if they are given a chance. However, in a land where only five percent of cheetah cubs make it to adulthood, there are no guarantees. "Obey today, eat today, live today" is the reality. Obedience is *required.*

A kill or be-killed existence, as old as the African plain on which the female cheetah hunts, sowed the seeds of obedience among the offspring of predator and prey. Fertilized with time and blood, it blossomed and bore fruit that nourished the perpetuity of both. In telling her cubs to remain where they are and not to make a sound until she returns, the cheetah is protecting them and the success of her hunt. Movement and unnecessary noise on their part will alert not only the gazelle she hunts but also the lion or hyenas that will be hunting her cubs. Glancing over her shoulder at the cubs before she vanishes into the long grass, she knows they will obey her in the same way as she obeyed her mother. *"It is my will you obey me, and my will is law."* Obey today, eat today, live today. Obedience is *required.* In the wild, the message is the same.

Like cheetahs, wolves are subjected to the same kill or be-killed rules that govern the cheetah's existence and thereby requires the same strict obedience from their offspring if they are to have any chance of making it to adulthood. Wolf cubs are subjected to discipline at a very early age. If they harass their mother because they are hungry and try to force her to feed them, she will grab them by their muzzles and pin them to the ground. She will not harm them, but the message, "*I will feed you when I am ready to feed you*," will not be lost in translation. They are taught, before it's too late, that the will of their parents is law and that any disobedience will be dealt with instantly and with physical punishment. Obey today, eat today, live today. Obedience is *required.*

Unlike the cheetah cubs that will leave their mother and become primarily solitary predators upon reaching young adulthood, wolf cubs that are social predators will remain with their parents long after reaching the same age. A condition of being a social predator is that it does not allow one to obtain the lofty goal of adulthood while shirking the childhood responsibility of obeying those superior to it. If it were allowed, chaos would quickly ensue as the adult wolf pack would begin to resemble any organizational unit that has too many bosses and not enough subordinates. Cooperation and compromise would be thrown out the window and replaced with "*my way or the highway!*" If that were to happen, the only thing hitting the highway would be the species known as *canis lupus*!

Old man winter does not allow wolves to profit from such an attitude. He covers their landscape with several feet of snow and issues forth bitter cold and low light for up to nine months of the year; thus, the small creatures that can sustain wolves during the summer are sent into hibernation or the deep recesses of the subnivean space. This leaves the wolves with a very limited menu of large herbivores with sharp hooves and large antlers or extra large herbivores with sharp hooves and extra large antlers. Choosing either will require you to invite several cooperating wolves to dinner if you plan to eat with your body still intact.

Even with the addition of cooperating wolves, dinner is still not guaranteed. Any chance of success will require luck, precise choreography of individual attacks, and the type of teamwork that is obtained only when immediate and unquestioned responses on the part of the subordinates befit the will of the leaders. For any pack of wolves that fails to meet these requirements, this menu offers starvation as an appetizer and death for dessert. The message repeats itself: obey today, eat today, live today. Obedience is *required*.

This message of the wild has been tamped by mankind's beneficence to the dog for many centuries. As a result, pet dogs are not required to work in a coordinated effort or obey their owners to eat. I have had clients who owned the most dominant and obstinate dogs in the world. These dogs ruled their households and had their owners jumping at the slightest indication of a want on their part. They made living with them absolute Hell, and yet, their owners would forego personal luxuries to indulge their dogs with the most expensive dog food available. For these dogs, the message of the wild has changed a bit. Obey today, eat today, live today. Only now, it's their submissive owners doing the obeying, not them.

Today's domestic dog existence may not be governed as harshly as that of the wolf, but obeying is still the rule of the day. As direct descendants of the highly evolved social wolf, where the concept of equality among members provides no useful contribution to its survival, dogs are still held fast to this rule by nature. The linear hierarchy she infused in the wolf's being for its durability has been passed to our dogs. Until nature decides to let our dogs out of the deal, we need to accept the fact that we are not on an equal status with our dogs no matter how much we desire it to be so. There are no equal wolves, no equal dogs, and no equal dog-to-human relationships. Nature *requires* obedience. With that, we can either decide to maintain our status above our dogs and reap the rewards of having a pet that obeys us, or we can allow our dogs to achieve a status above us and suffer the misery of having a pet that doesn't obey. Either way, someone is going to be leading someone else regardless of the decision.

I had a client seek my advice in regard to her dog pulling her to the ground when she tried to walk it. I tried my best not to stare at her broken nose with two black eyes and the ugly scrapes on her hands, elbows, knees, and shins as she told me what happened. While she was attempting to walk her large, male hound, it had suddenly lunged at a squirrel and pulled her to the ground where it then proceeded to drag her on the pavement for several feet. I asked if this was the first time this had occurred. As she showed me a scar on her wrist, the result of a surgical repair, she said it wasn't. To my surprise, she then pulled up the sleeve on her other arm, revealing another scar, and said, "This was actually the first one!"

After taking a few seconds to digest what I had just heard and seen, I inquired if she had ever sought help in training her dog not to pull her. After the first incident, she tried the advice of a friend who told her to wrap her dog's leash around her wrist sufficiently enough to allow for only one foot of slack. Shortening the leash this way would prevent her dog from gaining enough momentum to pull her down. Perhaps, she may not have attempted such a foolish thing if she had watched a few rodeos with bull riders and observed how even though they tied one of their hands to the back of the bull for better control, they were still often violently thrown.

Her current injuries resulted from following the suggestion of a professional trainer who instructed her to stop in her tracks the second her dog started to go after a squirrel. She was then supposed to call her dog back to her while presenting a treat with the hand that obviously wouldn't be needed for holding onto the leash for dear life. Doing this would teach the dog that not pulling on the leash in pursuit of squirrels would earn it a delicious treat and thus solve the problem. A half second before her face impacted the pavement, my client realized squirrels trump treats.

Failure to *require* her dog to walk without chasing squirrels led to this client's devastating injuries. Because wolves and dogs will not continue to repeat any unsuccessful behaviors, her dog would have adjusted its walking conduct so as not to ever pull her to the ground if it had been given an adequate consequence for doing so. Instead, tactics such as restraint and bribery were introduced because the notion of imparting a physical punishment to correct her faithful companion's behavior did not sit well with the client. Unfortunately, weeks later, it took the fourth injury to motivate the client to *require* obedience from her dog.

Oddly, requiring obedience, with its inequality and its controlling effect, is not a concept lost to humans, who are another form of highly evolved social predators. From the beginning of time, man has needed man to bend to his will in order to survive. This ability to lead and control other men was not accomplished in the arena of politics and negotiations but rather in the coliseum of will and force. Without force, there is no bend; without bend, there is no hierarchy; without a hierarchy, there is no order; and without order, there is no survival. This is the way of all social predators, yet most dog owners today will try anything but force to achieve the desired behavior they want from the social predator they call their dog. Why is this? After all, because of their ancestral relationship with the wolf, the use of force to maintain control and create submission fits perfectly with the dog's *modus operandi.*

The answer lies with the vanishing will of Americans.

Perhaps because I grew up in a military household with a Special Forces tutor in an unforgiving land, I am biased when I say that America has grown soft. We were once good at using force to control our survival and freedom. Now, before any act of aggression is used, a lengthy and senseless process is required to obtain the approval of differing branches of government. Even when this is accomplished, the backlash of protesting Americans tempers the aggression that is necessary to achieve the desired results, thus leaving the door wide open for future antagonists that view us as weak.

This is not the way with wolves. When the dominant wolves of pack A discover a wolf from pack B trespassing on their territory, they will not convene a council or consider the opinions of their lower ranking pack members; instead, they will run it down and kill it. The wolf from pack B threatens the survival of the wolves from pack A by poaching their meager food supply. When you are a predator, living in the land of limited resources, the level of aggression that achieves the desired result leaves a thieving wolf dead.

Recently, I observed a mockery of the Gadsden flag so beloved by our military as a symbol of our country's fight for independence stenciled on the T-shirt of a young woman who was struggling to control her dog. It said, "Don't tread on me

... PLEASE." The woman's dog was acting wildly by pulling against its leash and howling at the top of its lungs because it wanted to get free in order to crash a soccer game being played a few yards away. Because the girl was failing miserably at her feeble attempts to restrain her dog, she turned to offering up a bargain. In her best "baby talk," she told her dog that if it stopped with its misbehaving, she would play ball with it later. Of course, the whining on her part only served to spur the dog on with more vigor. The soccer players, rightly believing the woman was about to lose her grip on her dog, began to pack up to leave the area.

To the girl's surprise, I walked over, grabbed the leash out of her hands, and gave it a good hard snap. Her dog immediately calmed down and sat quietly. Because the dog could sense my will, it looked up at me for further direction. "Geez, how did you get my dog to settle down so quickly?" the amazed girl asked. I replied, "Go home and erase the word "PLEASE" on the back of your shirt, and you'll be one step closer to figuring it out." Then, I turned and walked away. I had served proudly in our military, and I took offense to both the shirt and the woman wearing it, not because of her lack of dog handling skills but because of her lack of the essential ingredient necessary to control her dog in public so as not to disrupt a soccer game that was already in progress. That essential ingredient was will.

When wolves feel the need to adjust the behavior of another wolf, they do not offer up a bargain to achieve their will. Instead, they use a positive punishment, meaning they *give*, in order to immediately stop the undesired behavior of the other wolf and start the desired behavior. They do not use a negative punishment, meaning they *take away from*, because there simply isn't anything to take when you live life on the verge of starvation. The only option for taking is food and because they are social predators, that would have an immediate, unfavorable impact on both wolves' survival. In the wild, behavior adjustments on the part of social predators not only have to happen quickly, but they also have to happen period. The misbehavior of one wolf affects the survival of the whole pack.

Obey today, eat today, live today. Obedience is *required*.

Humans are one of the only creatures that will utilize a negative punishment to adjust the behavior of another human. We do this because we can. Unlike the wolf whose life is governed by the law of limited resources, most of our lives are governed by the law of vast resources. If we take a resource away from another human, unless it's food, shelter, or water, it won't affect his or her ability to stay alive. For example, taking my daughter's iPhone as a form of punishment does not have an unfavorable impact on my survival or hers, although she thinks she will die without it. I have my own iPhone. My life continues unhindered by the fact that my daughter can't use her phone. Other forms of negative punishment in my household and like many others include taking car keys, grounding, withholding allowance, taking away TV privileges, etc. Taking these resources and privileges often provides just the incentive necessary for our children to adjust their undesired behavior to the desired behavior.

Utilizing a negative punishment to achieve obedience works well in countries where the population has vast resources, but it doesn't work so well in those that don't. In the process of my studying predatory behavior, I have traveled to extremely poor, third world countries where the people live very wolf-like in that they live on the brink of starvation. Because there is nothing of value outside of food and water that can be taken from such people, these countries have had to resort to positive punishments such as caning, flogging, and even death to obtain obedience and order from their people. Mahatma Gandhi once said, "To a starving man, a piece of bread is the face of God." To such a person, a negative punishment such as being placed in a prison can become a means to stay alive. Sure, you may lose your freedom, but what good is freedom if it ends up starving you to death? At least in prison, you get to eat. Therefore, countries with starving masses have no use for negative punishments. Like the wolf, positive punishment is the rule.

Obey today, eat today, live today. Obedience is *required*.

Have you ever witnessed your dog employing a negative punishment to correct the behavior of another dog? No, you haven't. Why? As I have said many times in this book, dogs are domestic wolves, and their behavior is still dominated by that phylogenetic relationship. Wolves don't manipulate other wolves by utilizing negative punishments. If you answered "yes" because you saw your dog take a toy from your other dog, you are incorrect in your assumption. Your one dog took the toy from your other dog because he was the dominant dog and he wanted it, not because he was punishing the other dog. In fact, the dominant dog could not have cared less how the other dog felt about the taking of its toy. Because wolves don't pout or hold grudges, the dog that had its toy taken most likely shrugged it off and went in search of another suitable toy to chew on.

Have you ever witnessed a group of dogs, whether living together or just hanging out at the local dog park, making use of a positive punishment? Of course, you have. Why? Because dogs are domestic wolves, and they are governed by the same linear hierarchy that has been so instrumental in the survival of their ancestors. A linear hierarchy is an "I say, you do, or else" type of arrangement, and wolves will use the hammer to make certain it stays that way. At a dog park, this can be observed when a dog gets in the face of another dog that is uncomfortable with that particular intimacy. The uncomfortable dog's warning snarl is translated as, *"Get out of my space!"* I didn't create this hierarchical arrangement, and neither did you. Nature created it. She did so because she felt it was the best plan to ensure the stability and longevity of her social predators, and it obviously was, seeing how such predators, to include mankind, have survived and flourished in a world dominated by fierce competition for millions of years.

All of this being said, why would we, in our attempt to create a well-behaved dog, choose any training methodology that fails to imitate the method dogs use to adjust the behavior of other dogs? Why do we, instead, insist on using training methodologies that make use of reinforcers that dogs don't use or understand? Have we as humans become so arrogant that we feel we can relegate nature to the back of the bus while we take our place at the wheel? Nature is the architect of the proper training methodology for our dogs, and I believe our ignorance of such has fabricated the arrogance that has created a "know it all" creature in ourselves. As a result, today's dogs and their owners are suffering from this arrogance in the form of more leash laws, dogs being outlawed in a rising number of city and national parks, some breeds being banned in some states, escalating aggression to humans, rising cost in insurance, rising number of landlords forbidding dogs on their property, rising number of clinically maladaptive dogs, decreasing number of handlers and dogs competing in dog trials, and the list goes on and on.

Over the years, I have had to undo many levels of damage to dog owner relationships caused by veterinarians or trainers who advocate the use of a "positive only" methodology. No negative punishment, no positive punishment, no punishment of any sort is their way. Fluffy is to enjoy an unruffled existence in which good behaviors lead to treats, petting, and an abundance of attention, while bad behaviors result in a reduction of such or are simply dismissed as a result of the dog acting out because it hasn't been given enough treats or petting or attention by its neglectful owner. Seriously nothing, and I mean nothing, in this entire world works like that! As wonderful as this training concept sounds, it is bankrupt because such a concept is lost on dogs and wolves. If you are a predator on this planet, domestic or otherwise, nothing is free or free of consequences. Obey today, eat today, live today. Obedience is *required*. That is the rule.

The ability of these vets and trainers to peddle such an illogical and ridiculous philosophy to their clients is only made possible by the absence of will in their clients to do what is necessary to *require* obedience from their dogs. This lack of will is becoming more prevalent in our ever softening American society, and it has affected not only our control of our dogs but also the parenting of the younger members of our households. Everywhere you turn, there is evidence of such. The use of a positive punishment like paddling to adjust student behavior became extinct over thirty years ago. When I went to school, the "board of education" did not resemble anything like a governing body of people, but its positive effect on deterring unwanted behavior at school was undeniable.

Nowadays, instead of a paddle, a conference is arranged with the offending student's parents and a faculty member of the school where first, the parents are told about all of the great qualities their child possesses (in light of the fact that today's parents are unreasonably protective of their children, it's a good way to start). Then, strategies are discussed as to how to shore up any minor inadequacies (definitely a better choice of two words than juvenile delinquent) in non-academic behavior observed in the student. These strategies are promptly followed up with suggestions on implementation of such at home and during school. Great! Except there's one problem—the school's well thought out suggestions and strategies are being passed to the very individuals who lacked the *will* from the onset to do what was necessary with their child to ensure they would never have to receive those very suggestions and strategies.

To add to this, where kids used to receive letters of the alphabet for grades, they now receive numbers because we certainly wouldn't want to stress our little future leaders of America by giving them an "F" for their laziness and inept academic performance. When I saw this for the first time, I had to ask, "What the heck is a 3?"

I believe self-preservation, on the part of academic institutions, may have played a part in deciding to use numbers instead of letters in grading. After all, stressing a child leads to stressing the parents, who then take their stress out on the school for their inability to provide the quality of instruction necessary for their, obviously very intelligent, child to achieve passing scores. Never does it seem to cross these parents' minds that perhaps if they had the will to make their child stop playing video games and start hitting the books, they could have lessened some of the stress in their lives.

Whenever my wife and I talk to prospective clients who insist on "positive only" training experience, the first question we ask the client is, "Do you have children?" If the answer is yes, we tell them not to bring their children to their "not positive only" lesson with us. This is done for the client's benefit because past experience has proven that the concept of *requiring* obedience from our children has become lost to most parents, and we have had to spend more time correcting the behavior of such children when they attended the training sessions than spending actual time with the client's dog. Our desire is for our clients to have the ability to concentrate on learning how to instill high-spirited obedience in their dog instead of leaving the training session with the highest bill they have ever paid for one hour of babysitting.

If we cannot find the will to *require* obedience from our children, what chance do we have of *requiring* obedience from our dogs? At least with our children, as a minimum, you can make use of threat tactics. Even if you lack the will to follow through with the threats, they will suffice as temporary motivators for a few of them. However, because a dog's ability to learn stems from associating feedback with the input given, you would have to summon up the will to give the input if you wanted your future threat to mean anything to your dog. Case in point, most young domestic dogs that have not been socialized with a non-conspecific such as a cat will ignore the threatening hiss and arched back of the cat and wade right into a switchblade factory. However, later on when the dog comes across the cat again with its threatening hiss and arched back, it will be reminded of the painful gashes across its muzzle and back off. By utilizing nature's positive punishment method-ology, the cat achieves a reliable response from the dog to its threatening posture. Dog owners and parents would do well in modeling their output after the cat if they wish to achieve a reliable response to that output from their dogs and children. Threats without follow-through are just more noise in an already noisy world.

I have taught thousands of dog owners how to *require* obe-dience from their dogs. In doing so, I have counseled them and instructed them in the subtle ways of dominance and sub-mission and the humane and justifiable use of the hammer on their part. All of these enlightened owners went on to con-struct a successful and meaningful relationship with their dogs, and along the way, they learned a thing or two about their dogs and themselves.

First, they learned that acquiring the ability to call all of the shots would earn them the dog of their dreams and the harmo-nious relationship they craved. They learned that the acquisi-tion of such didn't require a positive punishment that resem-bled abuse, or aversive stimuli (as the "only positive" trainers phrase it). It didn't require screaming at their dogs or harsh leash corrections or choking their dogs to death either. It also didn't require isolating their dogs in a cage all day or the with-holding of treats and privileges such as walks or playing fetch. It simply required their use of the minimum level of positive punishment that was required to stop the undesired behavior in their dogs and start the desired behavior. This is exactly the way it's done by the wolves in the wild—nothing more and nothing less.

Secondly, they learned that their role as a leader to their dogs was not an option if they wanted to call all the shots.

Their dogs had already demonstrated they would and could take the top position without a thought given to how their prospective owner might feel about their demotion. In becoming the leader, they learned you didn't have to become a bully or a tyrant along the way. They learned that they had to be fair but firm in their leadership. Like the message conveyed by the mother cheetah to her cubs, there can be no room for negotiations. Most importantly, they learned about the incorruptible ingredient that nature requires of the leaders of her social predators. They learned *their* will must become law.

I wear many scars on my body that attest to the philosophy and methodology that dogs employ when they believe *their* will is law. At the time I received these painful wounds, I wished these dogs would have employed a negative punishment with me or at least offered up a few negotiable terms in their attempt to adjust my behavior. That was only wishful thinking because it didn't happen, and it's never going to happen. Most of these dogs had previously achieved a great deal of success in bending their owners to *their* will by their use of the hammer. All of these owners had tried anything and everything but the use of positive punishment to get control of their dogs, and they had failed miserably. Ashamed, wounded, and desperate, they brought their undefeated champions to meet another undefeated champion—me. Even though these champions got in the first bite, they lost the fight because I brought something to the battle they had not experienced with another human. I brought my own hammer.

To this day, I do not regret any of the scars I adorn on my body. They were a necessary part of convincing the unbelieving owners of these powerful dogs what was necessary to obtain and maintain an elevated status in their hierarchy. A hierarchy in which they would be able to call all the shots and not suffer through the painful day-to-day existence they had been previously experiencing. The scars I regret are the ones that adorn my heart, the ones that earned a spot every time a dog was euthanized out of convenience because its pathetic owner lacked the *will* to *require* the dog to behave. Then, there are the scars left by the dogs lying dead in the street because their owners lacked the *will* to *require* their dogs to come to them when called. Lastly, there are those scars that resemble all of the scars left on children's faces by dogs whose owners lacked the *will* to treat their dog like a wolf and *require* obedience. Instead, they treated their dog like any other member of the family and tried to win its good behavior by winning its good favor. Their lack of *will* in *requiring* obedience sent word of a vacancy at the top of the hierarchy and gave cause to the use of the hammer by the dog to *require* obedience from their child.

My heart is only so big, and the scars from thirty years of this profession have made me, on many occasions, reconsider whether I really want to stay in this game. After all, we all get the dog we deserve, don't we? How much good am I really doing? Then one day, while sitting on an emergency room bed and watching a doctor sew up my latest bite wounds, the owner of the dog who had sent me there walked into the room. He was an older man and carried himself like a man who had weathered a few of life's storms and could easily weather a few more. I liked him from the minute I met him. However, I wasn't given much time to get to know him because within minutes of his lesson starting, I was attacked by his dog and sent to the emergency room for medical treatment. After standing there for a few moments, he said, "I am terribly sorry my dog bit you. It was my fault." "How's that?" I asked. Sure, his dog was out of control, but I had already chalked the bite up to carelessness on my part. "I lack *will*," he said quietly while looking down at the floor. Hmmm! I had never been given that as an excuse by an owner before. But, before I could say anything, he went on, "I would like to think I had *will* at one time. I would like to think I had it when I served in Vietnam and when I raised my two boys after I buried their mother and thought I couldn't go on without her. I would like to think I had it when I beat my last round of cancer and when I had my farm taken away by Uncle Sam because I couldn't pay my medical bills. But now, I don't think I have it anymore." Damn! Now it was my turn to look at the floor. Just a few minutes earlier, I had been feeling sorry for myself and thinking perhaps a new occupation was in line. Now I was disgusted with myself because the very definition of *will* was standing at the foot of my bed apologizing to me! Geez, even the doctor had stopped sewing! This was bad! "If I still had *will*," he continued, "I would have put my foot in that dog's butt like I did to my two boys a long time ago, and I wouldn't be needing to stand here and apologize to you for a lack of it." His eyes had lifted from the floor and were now boring holes through me. "You've got *will*, son. If you didn't, you wouldn't have been able to get my dog off of you as fast as you did, and you, for sure, would not have been able to get him under control with your arm all chewed up like that." I had no answer. All I could do was nod. "Never lose your *will*, son. If you do, you need to quit doing what you're doing." With that, the old man reached over and shook my good hand, thanked me, and walked out the door.

Obey today, eat today, live today. Obedience is *required*. Find your *will*.

Difficult Decisions

I am tired of fighting. Our chiefs are killed.
Looking Glass is dead. Toohulhulsote is dead.
The old men are all dead.
It is the young men who say yes or no.
He who led the young men is dead.

It is cold, and we have no blankets.
The little children are
freezing to death. My people, some of them,
have run away to the hills
and have no blankets, no food.
No one knows where

they are—perhaps freezing to death.

I want to have time to look for my
children and see how many I can find.
Maybe I shall find them among the dead.

Hear me, my chiefs. I am tired.
My heart is sick and sad.
From where the sun now stands,
I will fight no more forever.
~ Chief Joseph

The young elk calf struggles to stand, but his broken leg won't support his weight, and his other legs can't find traction in the frigid water rushing beneath him. Leaning against a large rock, he cries for his mother, a large cow standing near him, but her attention is on the nine wolves that occupy both sides of the narrow creek she tried to cross earlier with her calf. Their predicament apparently was the result of trying to make the treacherous crossing at a near gallop because they had been separated from their herd and were being pursued by the wolves. Normally, any attempt to cross such a creek in the early spring with its fast moving water and chunks of ice slamming into its crossers would require a near stop-and-go pace with total concentration on footing. However, tracks in the snow and mud leading up to the creek told of a pursuit by the wolves that was nearing a desperate end when the cow and her calf rushed headlong into the water.

While several of the wolves frantically pace back and forth along the banks, a single, black male with flecks of gray in his coat sits motionless. Even though he is barely visible against the dark canopy of spruce behind him, his amber eyes give him away. The other wolves, who are young, impatient, and hungry, make foolish attempts to separate the cow from her calf. Two of them almost get their heads kicked in by the cow's sharp front hooves before they wisely settle into just pacing the banks.

This is the black male's ninth winter, and surviving the pitiless cold for over eighty months has infused in him a quiet calm that comes with knowing that at the end of this day, patience will grant you a meal. Sitting a little heavier on his haunches, he disregards the conduct of the other wolves and locks his gaze on the cow. As the afternoon wanes and his shadow crawls out of the darkness behind him and lengthens to the East, his gaze has not wavered. The calf has stopped crying, and the cow's confident leer has taken on a look of defeat. For the first time, the cow glances over her shoulder to a stand of trees further up the creek where there are no wolves.

The black male, seeing this, slowly stands and stretches his muscles. He knows the time is near. The other wolves, aware that he has moved, stand as well and look at him in eager anticipation. As their leader, he knows they will not move until he is ready, and to drive home this point, he stands still for several more minutes. Then, satisfied with their obedience, he slowly advances to the edge of the creek and narrows his eyes on the cow. He is telling her, *"If you wish to live, leave now."* The cow, sensing the approach of certain death, steals one last look at her calf and then bolts for the stand of trees.

The black male watches her fading form for a few moments and then shifts his gaze to the calf as he steps into the icy water. The calf's desperate cries for his mother are drowned out by the sound of the other eight wolves rushing into the creek.

I have recounted this story to many of my clients over the years and have received a mixed bag of responses. Most feel sorry for the calf while others are amazed and disgusted by the cow's actions. They find it hard to believe that she could abandon her calf, and this is understandable. I have never found myself in the same predicament as the cow, but I would like to think I would do the heroic thing and fight to the death for my family. However, nature put the good of her species in the wild before personal emotions several millennia ago. Long before the black, male wolf advances to the edge of the creek, the cow knows what the outcome of the day will be. It is only the protective instinct that comes with giving birth to the injured calf that keeps her there until the end. But alas, when the end does come, she makes the difficult decision to abandon her calf so she can live to give birth to more elk.

For nature, it's not only the right decision, it's the only decision. The elk population benefits every time a decision like this one is made. The weak, deformed, and injured die and feed other animals while the herd is thinned enough to allow ample food for the healthy elk that possesses the stronger genes. For social predators, herbivores, or ungulates, it's never about the one—it's about the many.

In America, we don't possess the same strategic ideology as nature. No thought is ever given to the many because we're too determined to save the one at all costs. With the number of "no-kill" shelters and rescue agencies continuing to rise in the United States, we are saving animals that nature would have killed. As a result, the species, *canis lupus familiaris,* is suffering from it, along with the humans that coexist with them. This claim is a personal opinion of mine but is based upon thirty years of experience dealing with ever increasing problems associated with weak genetic baselines, poor human decision-making, and what has been clearly presented in the wild by nature. To prove the latter, next time you make a trek into the outermost regions of Alaska, Canada, or the Pacific Northwest, let me know if you come across a veterinary hospital or a Walgreens Pharmacy. I am confident you won't because nature has no need for them. Culling the weak, nonproductive members is an essential part of the process required to keep nature profitable and in the black, not in the red.

In the wild, wolves with dominant genes are the only wolves to breed within a pack. Usually, it is only the alpha male and the alpha female. However, in the case in which a female other than the alpha has a litter, she is normally the most dominant female below the alpha. Wolves with submissive genes are not allowed to mate within the pack.

By making this exception to breeding, in regard to submissive wolves, nature is assured that the best possible gene pool, derived from the strongest, brightest, and most willful wolves, is passed on to the next generation. There are many other factors that play into the successful continuance of any species, but this move, above all others, stacks the deck in nature's favor for her wolves because those animals that possess stronger genetic baselines have proven their ability to survive in conditions that weak genetic baselines don't.

One winter day, while hunting hares as a young boy in Alaska, my Special Forces mentor was shot through his neck when his .22 caliber rifle accidentally discharged. I was amazed at his calmness as he assessed the damage with no sign of panic or concern for the blood that seeped from both the entry wound and the exit wound. After a few moments of physical inspection, he winked at me, and with a controlled demeanor, he took off his pack and rummaged through it for his first aid kit. Finding what he was looking for, he quietly said with a grin, *"Sorry, kid, that was the last shot of the day."* He then proceeded to wrap a length of gauze around his neck.

It was going to be a very difficult three-mile trek back to the truck we had parked by the Chena river. The late spring had left a surplus of snow too watered down for snow shoes, so each step required high knee lifts and hard pulls to get any-where. At a few hours and half the distance back, I noticed the gauze around my mentor's neck was saturated with blood, and his breathing, which on most occasions was barely discernible compared to mine, was becoming more and more labored. I summoned up the courage to ask him if he wanted to stop. I told him I would go the rest of the way and bring back help.

With that, he paused and turned to face me. Sweat was pouring down his face, and I had never seen him look at me the way he was looking at me then. It was not just a mere threatening look but something far more deadly than anything I had seen previously from my mentor. *"If you were me, what would you do?"* he hissed. I'm not sure I saw his lips move when he asked the question, so before I realized he did and could answer, he asked another one by saying, *"Would you send a boy that was too young to walk over a mile in these con-*

ditions by himself to a truck that he was too young to drive the thirty hazardous miles needed to get help in the last thirty minutes of available daylight?" I'd had too many lessons with my mentor to know that kind of question only had one answer. "No sir," I replied. *"I am like the alpha wolf. I am your leader and your teacher. What lesson about survival would subordinate wolves or what would you learn if their leader sat down and quit?"* This question was one of those that did not require an answer from me, so I kept my mouth shut and tried not to blink. He went on, *"The wounded wolf has only one difficult decision to make in regard to a circumstance like mine. Either move and live, or lie down and die. I have seen it many times out here, and it's the strong wolf that chooses to move and the weak wolf that chooses to lie down."* My mentor paused a moment to let this latest lesson sink in, and then he asked, *"Which wolf are you?"* I bit my lip and fought desperately not to cry. With the most confident voice I could muster at that moment, I answered, "I am the strong wolf." After a few moments, his gaze softened its hard stance and turned to curiosity. It was as though he was searching for a secret that was deep inside of me. As he did, my mind raced to the past few years I had spent with him in hopes that some revelation would uphold my answer. But no help came my way. My mentor was to be the judge, jury, and executioner of my fate at that moment, and I looked down as I waited for the gavel to strike. *"Ok then, kid, lead the way to the truck before I bleed to death."* When I moved past him to take up a position I had held only once before, I felt his strong left hand grab my backpack. As we trudged our way in the increasing darkness and cold, his hand remained there. Like the strong wolf, my mentor moved and lived.

A strong genetic baseline creates an animal with sustaining power. It finds the will to move and live and persevere while the same conditions cause the recipient of a weaker genetic baseline to lie down and die. Therefore, a strong genetic baseline, created by strong, dominant breeding, is essential to the survival of a species like the wolf who must deal with harsh conditions and a multitude of competitors fighting for a limited supply of food for its entire life. Without such a strong genetic baseline, the wolf wouldn't stand a chance in today's world.

Many so-called authorities on the subject argue that today's domestic dog does not have to possess a strong genetic baseline like the wolf to survive and perpetuate its kind because we are their benefactors and we provide them with ample food, shelter, and pharmaceuticals to keep them alive and healthy. Technically, these authorities are correct in their claim, but like the starving man mentioned in the previous chapter, what good is freedom if it starves you to death. What good are we doing the dog by making it totally dependent upon us for its survival? What good will have been done for the dog if we end up creating a species that is literally on life support? I think a question that begs to be asked is the following: is it a biological doll that we really want or a dog? It's already a tough enough road for the domestic dog when you consider the biological fact that most species mutate backwards instead of forwards on their own.

When I was the young boy that I mentioned earlier in this chapter, I honestly did not know of any dogs that suffered from storm phobias, fear aggression, tail chasing, fly snapping, separation anxiety, or the like. Additionally, I certainly did not know of any that had to have an antidepressant or anxiolytic psychotropic drug prescribed to them. Perhaps their owners did but not them. Nowadays, however, I evaluate at least fifteen to twenty dogs per week to determine if they suffer from a maladaptive use of aggression, and I evaluate the same number of dogs per week to determine if they suffer from a maladaptive condition that causes a continual and unwarranted fear that often leads to pathological stress if left untreated. If either case is determined to be maladaptive, I develop a pharmacotherapy program and team with the dog's veterinarian to administer the likes of Clomipramine, Amitriptyline, Fluoxetine, or Busiprone to help achieve a manageable state in regard to their prospective condition. The sad part is that I have kept up this pace for fifteen years. For the ten years prior to that, I evaluated a third of that number, and for the five years prior to that, less than a fourth. In other words, the psychological and physiological welfare of the domestic dog in America is worsening with each passing decade. This is the unfortunate result of an increase in a weakening gene pool brought about by intentional and unintentional breeding of dogs with extremely weak genetic baselines.

Unlike the wolf, weak and fearful domestic dogs in America are given the green light to mate and pass their feeble genes onto their offspring. The consequences of such breeding practices are sending the domestic dog into a deadly free fall.

I have given seminars on the weakening genetic baseline of the domestic dog to breeders of all experience levels. These breeders ranged from the full-time professional to the occasional backyard breeders to the one-time breeder that only wanted to produce a replica of their good old dog, Buster.

One of the top reasons some of these breeders claimed to adding more dogs to our world was their personal need to contribute to the betterment of the breed they bred. Their intentions may have appeared to have been quite noble on the surface, but the pups they produced often failed to better anything to include their own kind or the humans that took them in. Had these breeders been more knowledgeable about the inner workings of canine genetics, had they learned how to recognize the traits exhibited by dogs with dominant genes, and had they been able to stand outside their own personal biases, they would have, like nature, stacked the deck in favor of their breed. Not every hand would have been a winning hand, but these breeders would have left with more money in their pockets than what they came with.

Because having too many dominant wolves upsets the balance nature strives for with her stable strategy, she will not always throw aces and kings. Low cards and even the occasional deuce keep the hierarchy from becoming too top heavy where the existence of too many potential leaders would create a blood bath for supremacy instead of the necessary teamwork required for survival. For this reason, the concern that breeders have with breeding only dominant dogs is without merit; they believe that by doing so, their puppies would all have dominant genes, grow to be too much to handle by their customers, or become too aggressive. Even in the wild, where breeding is much more deliberate and controlled to ensure only dominant wolves breed, nearly an equal number of submissive wolves are produced.

Dominant + Dominant = Dominant/Submissive = Perfect!

Given that when nature breeds only dominant wolves and submissive wolves (who are more insecure than dominant wolves) are still produced, imagine what happens when we go against nature and breed submissive genetic baselines to submissive genetic baselines? Submissive + Submissive = Not Perfect! That's what happens! Nature never intended for her social predators to breed Submissive + Submissive. That's the surest and fastest route to the town of "Past Tense" that the animal kingdom knows of, and yet it happens nearly every day in America! Breeding a very insecure submissive dog to another very insecure submissive dog will result in some pups running around that will perceive normal, every day activities and those living things participating in them as threats. Others will develop a maladaptive dependency upon their owners or the other dogs in the family, and some will develop compulsive behavioral disorders such as fly snapping, star gazing, or tail chasing. Add to this all the reinforcements that life with humans will provide to make their conditions worse such as loud noises, abusive care, abandonment, misperceptions, and faulty decision-making, and it's no wonder the pharmaceutical industry smells money!

When it comes to dog breeding, we have to pay due diligence to the process. We have to abide by nature's rules and place our trust in her plan. We can't just haphazardly mate two dogs because of how they look, because they worked out well for you and your household, because they have show titles, because you want a clone of your previous dog, or because you want to be the first to come up with the next designer dog breed and give it a cool name. If we truly want to benefit the domestic dog species with our breeding practices, then we have to put our emotions and our profits aside and make the difficult decision to breed only those dogs that carry the trait of dominant dogs: confident, stable, and strong, regardless of how we feel about the dog(s) being bred. If we can find the will to do this, we will someday come to enjoy the companionship of an animal that will never have unwarranted fears, phobias, or OCDs and need the help of a psychotropic drug just to make its life somewhat bearable.

Orchestrating a strong genetic baseline comeback, by implementing nature's breeding plan, is the first step in restoring the domestic dog's mental and physical stability that is required to ensure their behavior is compatible with the human race. The second step includes making difficult, but correct, decisions regarding domestic dogs that have already been born.

A "no-kill" policy instituted by some animal shelters and rescue groups equates to a "no-chance" policy when it comes to ensuring that the domestic dog's future behavior will have the needed stability to become compatible with the human race as mentioned in the previous paragraph. If a dog is so maladaptive in its use of aggression that it is beyond the help of a pharmacotherapy program, what do these organizations do with the dog if they don't kill it? Do they provide it with donated dog food and a shelter that comes in the form of a 3 x 5 foot kennel for the next ten to twelve years until it dies of old age? Or, do they attempt to rehabilitate it by bringing in a behavioral therapist who tries to instill in it a more rational use of aggression? Or, do they simply allow some poor, naive sucker to adopt the dog like one rescue group tragically did with a lady who came to me for help with her upcoming court case. The actions of her newly acquired Pit Bull from a "no-kill" rescue had led to the death of another dog and the disfigurement of its owner, and now she was in legal hot water and fighting for her financial life.

The lady I speak of had just recently retired from thirty-five years of service with a major corporation. Two months prior to her retirement, her husband of forty years had passed away and left her with a life insurance policy pay out that, coupled with her 401k and savings, would leave her with the financial means to move to a house on a sunny beach somewhere and spend the rest of her life without worrying about money. She was all packed and ready to go when a well-meaning friend persuaded her to adopt a dog and take it with her. Her friend had convinced her that the dog would not only provide a form of protection, but its companionship would also help her cope with those lonely nights without her husband. With her friend accompanying her, the lady visited a local "no-kill" Pit Bull rescue one morning where she adopted a three-year old male that had been described to her by the staff as a "big baby that would repel any bad guys, including any of those that would be asking her for a date!" Laughing, the rescue staff went on to tell her that the dog was also very well socialized and was obedience trained and, therefore, would be a cinch for her to handle while walking on the beach together.

Later that afternoon, while the lady and her newly adopted dog were taking their first walk, they encountered another lady walking her Yorkshire Terrier. The rescued Pit Bull, upon seeing the Terrier, immediately pulled away from his new, unsuspecting owner and launched an attack. The Terrier's owner screamed at the Pit Bull and kicked it repeatedly in an attempt to save her dog that was being torn apart by the Pit Bull. Before the Pit Bull's new owner could reach the bloody scene, the dog finished killing the Terrier and turned his attack on the lady who was kicking him and tore out the woman's right calf muscle.

A rescue group with a "no-kill" policy and a negligent adoption practice was to blame for this tragedy, but it wasn't any of the rescue staff that lost their dog or their ability to ever walk unassisted again. It also wasn't any of the rescue staff who lost their entire life savings to the victim and her personal injury attorney; to make matters worse, they won't have to worry about having the gory visual images of the incident, filled with screams of anguish, replayed over and over again in their heads for the rest of their lives. No sir. Their "do gooder" lives will go unhindered as they smile and congratulate one another each time another killer is saved and adopted. In a bit of twisted irony, the "big baby" the "no-kill" rescue group refused to kill was killed by authorities two weeks after it killed the Terrier and killed any quality of life for these two women.

Another painful case involves the attack on a six-year-old girl by a Golden Retriever adopted from another "no-kill" rescue group. The girl's parents, wanting to surprise their daughter on her sixth birthday, called upon the retriever rescue group to assist them in adopting the perfect dog to give to their daughter who had always wanted a dog. After reviewing the mandatory questionnaire that was answered by the girl's parents, the rescue group quickly located the ideal dog for their daughter. Even though the dog had been rehomed three previous times for biting adults, the incidences were explained away by the rescue group as the result of ignorant and neglectful adopters that had obviously mistreated the dog. The parent's initial concerns were quickly dispelled as they witnessed how affectionate the dog was to its loving adult foster and the added assurance that "children don't pose a threat to dogs like neglectful adults; therefore, this dog would never have a reason to bite your daughter."

The presentation of the new dog was a huge success at the girl's birthday party, so much so, that most of the girl's other presents went unopened because she was so caught up in petting and talking to her new best friend. When the party finally ended and it was time for the girl to go to bed, she begged her parents to let the dog sleep with her. The parents, seeing no harm in allowing the new dog to sleep with their daughter, quickly approved and giggled in delight as they watched their six-year-old skip off to bed with the new family dog in tow.

Congratulating each other on selecting the perfect dog for their daughter, they turned their attention to cleaning up after the party. What they had failed to notice were the two cookies their daughter had taken with her to bed. The dishwasher wasn't fully loaded before their daughter's agonizing screams filled their home.

I met with the girl and her parents two months after the incident occurred. The girl had just recently been released from the hospital, and bandages still covered most of her left arm and the left side of her face. When I bent over and shook her tiny right hand, she tried to smile, but the scar tissue at the corner of her mouth only allowed a slight grin. I couldn't take my eyes off her as she stood looking up at me with her grin remaining. There was something so wrong about a girl being injured like this by a dog, but there was something so right about how she seemed at the moment. Curious, I asked her, "So, what's up with all the grinning?" After all, this little girl had just left a hospital after spending over a month there because she had been mauled by her birthday present. *"My mommy and daddy said you will help me get a new puppy that won't hurt me when I give it a cookie. They said you would because I did so well while I was in the hospital. Will you?"* she asked hopefully. I stole a quick glance in the direction of her parents and noticed the girl's mother was crying. I was awed by the family's courage and the faith they had placed in me. Turning back to the little girl, I dropped to one knee and confidently answered, "I will," because I knew nature still produced dogs that didn't feel the need to try to kill a little girl over a cookie in bed.

Sadly, these are just two stories out of hundreds that I have been involved with over the years. Even sadder is the fact that all of these could have been avoided if those who were in charge of placing these deadly dogs with families or individuals had made the difficult, but right decision to euthanize them before the authorities had to. Nature certainly would have. She has no place in the wild for animals possessing maladaptive aggression or fear. She would have cleaned her house and swept them out the door of existence.

Everyone, from animal shelters to rescue groups to PETA (People for the Ethical Treatment of Animals) to the ASPCA (American Society for the Prevention of Cruelty to Animals) to breeders to ordinary dog owners, wants to take a part in saving our dogs. They all give incredible sums of time, money, and energy in their fervent pursuit of a dream where every happy American family enjoys the companionship of a happy, tail-wagging dog. But, like the deadly and undetectable carbon monoxide gas that lulls its victims into a never ending sleep, their dream-like focus on saving the one has allowed the many to fade from their consciousness into a deepening and enveloping darkness.

If there is to be any chance of turning the dream into reality and pulling the domestic dog from the deepening abyss, we must find within the human heart the ability to make the difficult decisions that come with any responsible stewardship. We must turn to nature and her wisdom and model our charge after hers. That means we must abandon the "no-kill" mindset and develop a "kill with the utmost discrimination" mindset. We must have the courage to go against the beliefs held most popular by those who lack the knowledge and the will to do what is necessary for the many, including euthanizing the one that is incapable of conforming safely with mankind.

Contrary to how I come across in this chapter, I am very grateful for the work that animal shelters, rescue groups, and individuals do in saving those dogs that are capable of conforming safely with mankind. I am also very grateful to those breeders who do everything they can to produce dogs as nature intended and, thereby, are looking out for the many. I believe the success of these shelters, groups, and breeders is due in part to their knowledge of canine behavior and genetics. That being said, I am not grateful for the rescue groups, individuals, or breeders that use the "save the dog campaign" as a platform to elevate their own personal status and exalt their own personal beliefs. Their bulldogged convictions, such as "no-kill" at all cost, allow no room for rebuttal of any sort. They're right, and everyone who doesn't agree with them is wrong. Instead of making the difficult decision to become more open minded and more knowledgable about canine behavior and genetics and the positive effect it would have on the dogs they want so desperately to save, these individuals and groups throw caution to the wind and just wing it.

Perhaps winging it will get you by with a lot of things in this life, but when you just wing it with a maladaptive dog, a human is harmed, and a dog is killed.

The many. It's what nature intended for the continuance of wolves. The many. It's what nature intended for the continuance of dogs. This must become our mantra. The many. This must become our credence. The many. This must become our duty. The many. We took the dog from the wild where nature would have protected it, nurtured it, and continued it, and in the process, she would have kept it healthy, stable, and full of life. Now, it is our responsibility to safeguard the dog's future by putting their future before our personal beliefs and desires. To accomplish this, we will have to make many difficult decisions on behalf of the many or make the difficult, future decision of who gets to own the one... that's left.

The cow slows her pace long after she is unable to hear the dying cries of her calf. Exhausted, her lungs burning and her vision faltering, she scans the deepening, twilight shadows behind her for any sign of pursuit by the wolves. Detecting none, she turns and continues her urgent and difficult journey.

The night has brought a chilling wind that is freezing the melting snow under her hooves and hindering her progress, but she continues for she knows safety from the wolves is measured by distance.

Finally, when the moon has settled low on the horizon, she is spent and can move no further. Finding a patch of bare ground on the high bluff she has climbed, she lowers her weary frame to the ground. Even though she fights desperately to remain alert, exhaustion soon overcomes her, and she lapses into a deep sleep.

In her sleep, her calf calls for her. In her sleep, she does not hear the terrifying sound of the wolves; she only hears the calling of her calf. It is not a call for help or a voice of anguish and suffering. It is simply the mew he had given often when she had strayed too far for his comfort or when her pace had been too fast for him to keep up. The cow gave birth to this calf, and she knows his mew from a thousand other calves. This mew she hears in her sleep is his.

The cow snaps out of her unconsciousness and answers with a long, mournful mew of her own. It is a wounded sound that tells of a despair that nature knows all too intimately. Before it settles on the valley below, the cow realizes her calf is not with her. The cry she heard was only in her sleep. Realizing this, she lies there for several painful minutes hoping to hear his mew again, but when only the wind calls, she stands, shaking off the frost that has covered her coat, and casts her gaze on the distant mountains silhouetted by the early rays of the morning sun. There, at the foot of the mountains, is where she will find her herd and where she will renew her purpose in life. Before long, she will hear the mew of the newborn elk that will replace her calf. She is a strong cow with an indomitable spirit and will that is born of a genetic baseline created by nature to withstand the effects of the difficult decisions required to survive in the wild. Casting her snout into the cold, blowing wind, she momentarily checks for signs of the wolves or other danger before beginning her descent. When all that is detected is the smell of damp earth and the raucous caw of a raven, she lets out a mew. It is a soft and quiet mew that can barely be heard above the creaking pines, but its tender message is carried by the wind until it settles on a large rock in an icy creek several miles away. Then, keeping the distant mountains ahead of her, she moves and lives.

The Path of Two Prints

Hold on to what is good,
Even if it's a handful of earth.
Hold on to what you believe,
Even if it's a tree that stands by itself.
Hold on to what you must do,
Even if it's a long way from here.
Hold on to your life,
Even if it's easier to let go.
Hold on to my hand,
Even if someday
I'll be gone away from you.
~ Pueblo Prayer

I stood there dazed and confused. The bad news had come suddenly and without warning just the day before. Dressed in his starched fatigues, polished jump boots, and his green beret draped over the top of his right ear, my mentor stood a few yards away talking to his wife and two daughters who were crying. Looking back and forth from him to the large duffle bags on the sidewalk, I couldn't believe he was leaving. Alaska had always seemed too small to hold him. He was larger than her mountains and twice as strong. Now, Alaska was going to be an impossibly big and lonely place without him. My mentor was being shipped off to Vietnam.

This man had been more than a teacher to me. He had been my inspiration and my source of drive—a real life hero and the man that I wanted to be someday. I was having a difficult time deciding how I was going to make it in the world without him there to guide me. I couldn't stand to look at his packed bags any longer, so I dropped my head and stared at nothing.

"Hey, kid. What are you doing looking at your feet? Anything dangerous would have already been there before you ever saw it. Lift your head and look at the world. That way, you'll notice it before you step on it." I couldn't help but grin. My mentor always had advice to give, regardless of the circumstance.

"Let's me and you go for a walk," he said as he wrapped his all too familiar arm around my shoulders the way he had done a hundred times before. What was I going to do without his embrace? At that thought, I lost my composure and dropped my head back down to hide my tears.

"While you're looking down there, kid, do you notice how this path now has two sets of prints on it?" Looking behind us, I noticed the impressions left by my worn hiking boots and the

deep stenciled marks of his jump boots. "Yes sir," I managed to mumble.

"If a dog and a wolf walked next to each other on this path like us, would they not leave two sets of prints?" he asked. I managed another "Yes sir" as I wiped my nose.

"You know there is a wolf inside of every dog, right?" Another "Yes sir."

"Then if a dog were to walk on this same path by itself, would there not still be two sets of prints?" This time I answered with a "huh?" I was puzzled by the question but even more puzzled as to why my mentor had chosen such a rotten time for a riddle. After all, my world was coming to an end, and he was casually asking me questions that didn't make any sense. But, before I could voice my complaint, he went on to explain.

"An Indian chief explained this to me when I was your age. Because a dog carries a wolf inside of him, he also carries the wolf's prints. The wolf goes with him everywhere he goes. The impressions left on the earth by a passing dog are both a dog print and a wolf print. When an Indian walks a path beside his dog, their prints are two but remain as three."

"Yes sir, I understand," I barely whispered. Truthfully, I still wasn't quite following him.

"Do you carry me and all that I have taught you inside of you?" That question brought me to a sudden stop. I did carry my mentor inside of me. Every touch, every lesson, every trip into the wild was as much a part of me as the blood that coursed through my veins. Every smile, every stern look, every nod of approval was seared into my very being. Like the wolf in every dog, my mentor's instinct had become my instinct. He would always be inside of me. "Yes sir, I do," I answered with as much bravado as I could muster at that moment.

"Then always remember this, kid. You will tread on many paths in this life. Some paths will be easy going. Others will be as difficult as that spring snow we hacked our way through with me bleeding all over the place from that damn hole in my neck. Some paths will have many forks in them and will make no sense to you. That's when you will pull out the compass that is your heart and you will find your way, the way I have shown you many times before. Many years from now, you will walk the path that will lead you into our beloved wild for the last time. Be sure to walk all of your paths until then like the wolf: bold, determined, true to your pack, and grateful for every day you are given. Lastly, always remember it is the strong wolf that moves and lives."

He paused then and placed both of his hands on my shoulders. I lifted my head and stood as straight as I could, the way I knew he would want to remember me. As I looked into his steel gray eyes for what would be the last time, he said to me, *"No matter which of these paths you tread in this life, it will always be a path of two prints. I will be there inside of you, walking the same path, just like the wolf and the dog."*

My mentor was not a philosopher, a psychologist, or a biologist. He was a social predator that was held by the same threads that nature created to bind all other social predators. He used the wolf as an example or as a metaphor in the majority of his teachings about life because he was a wolf himself, and he was in tune with the instincts that influenced and safeguarded their existence. He knew how they related to his life and to mine.

In his last parable of the path of two prints, my mentor demonstrated his love and concern for me by revealing this knowledge. Somehow, he knew he was not going to survive

Vietnam, so he wanted to leave me with a final message about nature that he knew I could relate to and would always take comfort in.

He knew that nature's will was in all things, even in death. He knew her plan was perfect and permanent and could be trusted to safeguard our existence, just like the wolves we both so dearly loved. He knew that even though millions of wolves had walked their final path into the wild for thousands of years, what was inside of all of them had remained to form the thread that connects them to today's domestic dogs. In a similar way, he knew what was inside of him would remain, long after he walked his final path into the wild, to form a thread that would connect the two of us forever.

The thread that connects wolves and dogs is instinct. It comprises many lessons created and taught by nature, learned by wolves, and passed to dogs. It protects and nurtures both species by giving them similar tools needed to survive and reproduce. It remains among the living even when the individual wolf or dog no longer does. It is not invisible; it is real. One only has to look at a domestic dog with an open mind, and the wolf inside will reveal itself. Nature never intended to hide this wolf, but we've been too busy looking at our feet instead of the world around us. Anthropomorphism was underfoot before we even knew it was there. Like a deadly snake, it bit us and injected venom in the form of an unrealistic perception of our dogs that is slowly killing the harmonic relationship that nature deliberately sowed for us. For the family dog in America, anthropomorphism is the final path into the wild.

Fortunately, there is an anti-venom for the association of dogs as humans, but this cure does not come in the form of newly invented treats, clickers, gentle leaders, no-pull harnesses, or citronella spray. Nor does it come in the form of negotiations, arbitrations, or bartering. Humanistic psychology or all-positive training methodologies are both as effective in treating the condition as a tourniquet made of tissue paper. There is only one way to save our domestic dogs from the certain death that anthropomorphism promises. That way lies with you and your willingness to change.

I remember counseling a woman with regard to her two-year-old male Cane Corso and his latest attack on a jogger. The bite was the dog's third, and it had sent the jogger to the hospital for medical attention. I spent over two hours explaining why the bite had occurred and what she would need to do to protect others from being attacked by her dog in the future. I taught her about her dog's use of mechanisms such as the hammer and what provoked them. I explained how her dog viewed its world differently than she did. I exposed her perception of her dog as a human and informed her that that was the root of the problems she was having in controlling her dog. I lectured her on how treating him more like a wolf than like a human was the key to successful ownership of her dog. When I finished, she burst into tears and cried, "He is NOT a dog or some wolf. He's my baby boy. He didn't attack that jogger; he just wanted to play. If the jogger had stopped and played with him, none of this would have happened. Any so-called expert could easily see that was the case!" This woman refused to change, and a few weeks later, her dog bit a fourth person and was euthanized by court order.

No doubt, change is hard. Especially when it affects you or someone you love. There's an old saying, "You can't teach an old dog new tricks." I have found that when that "old dog" happens to be me, it's even more difficult! However, I have always found the will to change when it was necessary for the preservation of me, my family, my dogs, or my way of life. My mentor always mentioned change and nature in the same sentence. He said nature knew she needed change to keep pressure on her wolves. By requiring her wolves to continuously adapt to her ever changing world, she made them stronger and more intelligent and better able to withstand the pressures of the future changes she would instill. Like nature, my mentor continuously pushed me. I had to adapt and change constantly to successfully overcome an onslaught of one challenge after another. If I ever failed at a challenge, he would make me get up and repeat it until I got it right; then he would warn me to get ready to meet the next challenge he was going to hit me with. I can still hear him saying, *"One of these days, life will knock you down hard. When that happens, try to land on your back because if you can look up, you can get up."* In his way, he was preparing me for the most difficult change that would soon occur in my young life. He was preparing me for a life without him.

If we love our dogs, even a tenth of how much my mentor loved me, we will find the will to change. We will do for them what they cannot do for themselves. We will shed our fear of the wolf and replace the fear with curiosity. We will acquire knowledge of their ways and the mechanisms that drive their behaviors, and we will search for these in our dogs. We will learn to see our world through the eyes of a wolf and curtail our personal perceptions. We will make our "will" known to our dogs and retake our position as alpha to our pack. We will find the courage to make the difficult decisions that will safeguard the many for centuries to come. And finally, we will come to embrace the *wild* in our dogs.

In the fall of 1971, I received word that my mentor had died in combat. They said he was a hero and that I should be proud, but none of that mattered to a twelve-year-old boy. Without him, I was in a blizzard with no compass. I was profoundly lost, and I didn't care if I found my way out or not. I cried for days until the tears came no more. Life had indeed knocked me down hard.

Perhaps it was because of self-preservation or perhaps it was because of the many challenges my mentor had imposed on me, but either way, I must have landed on my back because a month later, I looked up and got up. The first real snow of winter had dumped eight inches on the wilderness landscape when I suddenly had an overwhelming urge to leave the confines of my home. Strapping on my snowshoes and my pack, I took a quick bearing with my compass and headed out. I had only traveled a short distance when I heard several wolves howl. My brothers had been patiently waiting for me. I smiled for the first time in weeks and picked up my pace. Looking down at the trail I was leaving, I could feel my mentor's arm around my shoulders, and I sensed his approval. It was as he said it would be—a path of two prints, and it was headed into the wild.

End of the Journey

No man ever followed his genius till it misled him.
Though the result were bodily weakness, yet perhaps
no one can say that the consequences were to be regretted,
for these were a life in conformity to higher principles.
If the day and the night are such that you
greet them with joy, and life emits a fragrance
like flowers and sweet-scented herbs,
is more elastic, more starry, more immortal:
that is your success. All nature is your
congratulation, and you have cause
momentarily to bless yourself.
The greatest gains and values are farthest
from being appreciated. We easily come to

doubt if they exist. We soon forget them.
They are the highest reality... The true harvest
of my daily life is somewhat as intangible
and indescribable as the tints
of morning and evening.
It is a little star-dust caught,
a segment of the rainbow
which I have clutched.
~ Henry David Thoreau, *Walden, or Life in the Woods*

"A wolf, huh? Who would have ever thought Rex was a wolf?" My client was staring out the window as she pondered all that I had taught her about her dog and his ancestor, the wolf, and why he had attacked her grandson. "When I was a child in Alberta, Canada, we used to see wolves all the time. My father raised cattle and hated the wolves because they would often kill one of our calves and even a large cow occasionally, especially if it were an exceptionally cold winter. We didn't have much money back then, so any loss of our cattle was very hard on our family." Then, turning to look at me, she continued, "Because of my father, I also grew up hating wolves, so it's no wonder I never looked for one in Rex. It has always been more comforting to think of him as part of our family. But now, I can see the wolf in Rex, and everything that has happened, even though it has been tragic, makes perfect sense." With that, she nodded and turned to look back out the window.

My client had now come to realize that Rex never viewed her grandson as family. Because the child visited her only a few times a year, Rex had always considered him an alien to his pack. The alien was a non-threat to Rex when it crawled and when it first began to walk upright, but, with time, the alien grew to be much taller than Rex with much more animation and a much more persistent desire to seek direct contact. As an energetic four-year-old wanting to play with a dog, the grandson had suddenly evolved into a viable threat to Rex. The initial grace and tolerance that was extended to the grandson when he was perceived as a non-threat was violently revoked when the child wrapped his arms around Rex's neck and tried to climb on his back like a pony. Nature gave wolves the "hammer" to repel threats, and Rex's use of it was swift, deliberate, and natural. The puncture wounds to the grandson's face and the resulting ultimatum issued by his parents were the motivation behind my client's visit.

"Now that you walk the path of three prints with Rex, what will you do with this knowledge?" I ask.

Without taking her eyes away from the window, my client answers, "First of all, I am no longer going to put Rex to sleep." The conviction in her answer makes me want to smile, but I hold back. To know that she really understands, I need to hear more. "Secondly, I am going to bring my grandson's parents to meet you. They need to take the same journey I did so that they can understand why Rex bit their son. Lastly, I will embrace the *wild* in Rex and enjoy the few years I have remaining with him in peace. I will be forever respectful of the wolf inside him and teach my grandson to be the same."

My client pauses for several moments after this last statement. The afternoon clouds have parted, allowing slivers of light to pass through the window and play off her amber eyes that are fixed on something unseen. Whatever it is, it is a moment in time that is deeply private and known only to this woman. As I watch the sun rays slowly move across her weathered face, I can't help but feel I am an intrusion, and out of respect, I stand to leave the room.

"Your mentor was a wise man. You were blessed to have been taught by him," she adds. The suddenness of her affectionate statement catches me off guard; for a moment, I am taken back in time to my childhood in the Alaskan wild, and my throat constricts. As I turn to face her, she reaches out for my hand and whispers, "Rex and I thank you and so would my husband."

About the Author

Bryan Bailey grew up in the Alaskan wild under the tutelage of a Special Forces survival instructor where he gained the invaluable experience of studying the similarities of the social interactions of wolves in their packs and those of today's domestic dog. Bryan's lifelong pursuit of understanding the inner workings of the canine mind and other social predatory behavior has led him to explorations in the African plains, the jungles of Southeast Asia, and above the Arctic Circle.

Bryan and his wife, Kira, reside on the banks of the Mississippi River in Memphis, TN, with their children, dogs, and cats. Together, they own ProTrain Memphis and Taming the Wild. In their free time they enjoy excursions into the wild, traveling, and exploring new places.

Bryan is currently at work writing his next book, <u>The Hammer: Understanding Canine Aggression</u>. Visit him online at Tamingthe*Wild*.com.

Bibliography

1. National Animal Interest Alliance (N.A.I.A.) article, Colorado Task Force Found No Need for Wolfdog Ban, 01/09/2012.

2. Derr, Mark. *How the Dog Became a Dog: From Wolves to Our Best Friend,* The Overlook Press; 1 edition (January 29, 2013).

3. Gallagher, Danny. *Forget Sharks. These other animals are more likely to kill you,* C/NET report, 06/20/2015.

4. Yoffe, Emily. *No Pet For You. Want to adopt a dog or cat? Prepare for an inquisition at the animal rescue,* Slate.com article, 01/26/2012.

5. *U.S. News and World Report,* May 22, 2013

6. *The U.S. Trade Group,* March 2013

7. Lawrence, D.H. *The complete poems of D.H. Lawrence,* Viking Press; volume 1 (1971)

8. Derr, Mark. *How the Dog Became a Dog: From Wolves to Our Best Friend,* The Overlook Press; 1 edition (January 29, 2013).

9. United States Centers for Disease Control and Prevention, *Preventing Dog Bites,* May 18, 2015